Cillian Murphy: War Hero

Cillian Murphy: War Hero

BearManor Media

2025

Published in the United States of America by:

BearManor Media

1317 Edgewater Dr. #110
Orlando, FL 32804

bearmanormedia.com

Printed in the United States.

Typesetting and layout by PKJ Passion Global

ISBN–979-8-88771-669-5

Cillian Murphy: War Hero

History buffs and film fans alike will find great value in these pages as they explore the war genre's greatest ever movies, and some of its best performances. In particular, Cillian Murphy: War Hero will shine light onto the famous Irishman's career, the impact his work has made on some of the greatest war movies ever, and pieces of historical context with regard to each of his characters.

What's more, he also provided indelible efforts on television as Thomas Shelby, a veteran and war hero in the hit series *Peaky Blinders*, while also playing soldiers in both stage plays and short films. Across three mediums in total, Cillian Murphy has portrayed seven active-duty soldiers, two veterans, and an essential figure of World War II.

Foreword: A History of War Movies and the Genre's Best Actors

Since the dawn of the medium itself, some all-time great filmmakers have carefully painted the brutalities of war on the silver screens of cinema. Just as one example, take a look at Samuel Fuller. He's made some of the all-time greatest depictions of battle, such as *The Steel Helmet* (1953) and *The Big Red One* (1980). He's perhaps the foremost authority on the genre, not just because of the aforementioned titles, but also by dint of his serving in the Second World War.

An infantryman to the 16th Regiment, 1st Division, he traversed the trenches of WWII throughout Sicily, Africa, and Normandy, and for his service, Fuller was subsequently honored with numerous awards, from the Bronze and Silver Stars to the Purple Heart and Combat Infantryman Badge. To call him experienced would be putting Fuller's status as a war director in the absolute lightest of fashions, and although genre lines are fine, he once defined the category at hand for historians and pundits to reference.

According to Geoffrey Macnab of *The Independent*, the hardened veteran and famous filmmaker once said that, "a war film's objective, no matter how personal or emotional, is to make a viewer feel war." Simple enough, and with that being said, it's worth noting that Fuller is only scratching the surface of directors who are known for their war films.

Perhaps in more famous fashion—from widely recognized performers to more niche names of the industry—there are also plenty of actors who have become known for fighting on the battlefield. This is a common occurrence, actors being known for a particular type of title. It's by no means exclusive to war films. Dozens of examples could be touched on from the medium's most popular genres, like westerns, for instance.

The performer most commonly associated with westerns is John Wayne. He's essentially synonymous with the genre, having appeared in scores of films throughout his career that were set in the Wild West. Meanwhile, other examples of genre masters include Jamie Lee Curtis with horror movies, and Sigourney Weaver with sci-fi films. Now, thanks to his brilliant portrayal soldiers throughout various world conflicts, there's also Cillian Murphy: War Hero.

Precise accounts of the first ever war movie are difficult to pinpoint, though most film historians settle on *Tearing Down the Spanish Flag* (1898) as the original. A short, it runs for just over ninety-seconds, and from there, hundreds of shorts and feature-length films alike were released throughout the silent film era. Comedies with Charlie Chaplin, epic dramas about World War I—no matter the essence of the respective project in tone, style, or setting, the battlegrounds of war became a hotspot for actors since the youngest years of the medium.

Perhaps the most prominent from the early days of cinema was *The Big Parade* (1925), a scathing analysis of World War I. Director King Vidor captured various themes in the sights of his filmmaking rifle, like his protagonist taking aim at a squadron of Germans from within the trenches of France.

A highly revered take on the suffering of soldiers, *The Big Parade* influenced future genre movies such as *All Quiet on the Western Front* (1930). Quite the popular title, based on the novel of the same name by Erich Maria Remarque—and one of the earliest examples of a war film to be released within the pre-code era of Hollywood.

While other, well-known titles such as *Wings* (1927) feature prominent elements of the genre, the development of sound films brought about some of the truest representations of war that the medium had to offer. Take *La Grande Illusion* (1937), for instance. Often cited among the best movies ever made, *La Grande Illusion* was directed by Jean Renoir from a script he co-wrote with screenwriter Charles Spaak. One reason the film was so lauded around the world was by virtue of its realism, which can largely be attributed to the history of the filmmakers themselves—particularly, Renoir.

During WWI, he was a reconnaissance pilot, and he parlayed that experience wonderfully into directing his magnum opus. It tells the story of Captain de Boëldieu and Lieutenant Maréchal—played by Pierre Fresnay and Jean Gabin—aviators for the French during WWI who are shot down by German Imperial Army and taken to a prisoner-of-war (POW) camp. They befriend some fellow Frenchmen while held within captivity, and thus, they all band together to escape.

The movie received widespread praise, and across the board of its cast, everyone's acting was held in high regard, as well. Take Gabin, who went on to provide some explosive performances in several war movies down the line. After *La Grande Illusion*, he had a cameo in *Napoléon* (1955) as Marshal Jean Lenins, a military commander of the First French Empire, while a lesser-known war movie that featured Gabin as the lead was *The Imposter* (1944), which is set during World War II.

Another long-serving actor of war movies was Errol Flynn—in just four years, he appeared in five movies centered entirely around WWII. These were released throughout the conflict, too: Between 1942 and 1945, famous thespian Errol Flynn defined the genre alongside his greatest collaborator Raoul Walsh, who in turn is among the greatest director of the genre thanks to his pitch-perfect portrayals of the Second World War.

By far, that's the most represented conflict in cinema, with speculative numbers in that regard ranging upwards of a thousand. And of all of those movies set between 1939 and 1945, Irish actor Cillian Murphy has played characters in four of them. This isn't entirely uncommon, though the caliber of his performances undoubtedly fit that bill.

In the sixties, Charles Bronson appeared in multiple WWII movies, such as *The Great Escape* (1963) by John Sturges and *The*

Dirty Dozen (1967) by Robert Aldrich. Both were highly successful, lucrative at the box office and well-represented at the most prestigious award ceremonies that the industry has to offer, from the Golden Globes to the Academy Awards. There are several other actors among their respective casts worth noting, on top of Charles Bronson.

Bronson played supporting parts in both *The Great Escape* and *The Dirty Dozen*, two of the greatest war films ever. Let alone of the decade. In the former, Bronson co-starred alongside Steve McQueen, another war veteran of cinema. Also throughout the sixties, McQueen starred in titles such as *Hell is for Heroes* and *The War Lover*—both from 1962—that rendered him a household name, and a recurring soldier of cinema.

From that same decade, there's also *Dr. Strangelove* (1964), and speaking of: Its director Stanley Kubrick is one of the greatest directors the war genre's ever seen. His first (anti) war film, *Paths of Glory* (1957) is considered a cinematic masterpiece. He also directed *Full Metal Jacket* (1987) a couple of decades later. But back to the sixties: these pages would be entirely incomplete without the mention of *The Battle of Algiers* (1966), directed by Gillo Pontecorvo from a script by Franco Solinas.

Commonly cited among the greatest films ever made, *The Battle of Algiers* paints a picture of the eponymous excursion, but in the style of a newsreel, edited to appear as a documentary when it is in fact a work of fiction. This created an unrivaled sense of realism that few war films had seen before, while also giving the genre a chance to expand on the untamed prospect of guerrilla warfare.

Influential stuff, and it paved the way for one of the most prosperous periods in the history of war movies. For starters, just take a look at *Patton* (1970), directed by Franklin J. Schaffner. A widespread success both critically and commercially, *Patton* was written by Francis Ford Coppola. After his *Godfather* movies—and after other war movies like *The Deer Hunter* (1978), directed by Michael

Cimino—the all-time great Francis Ford Coppola would go on to create one of the greatest war movies ever.

Often cited among the finest films ever made, *Apocalypse Now* (1979) is without a doubt an all-time great when it comes to cinematic depictions of battle. It also features an all-star cast of on-screen veterans, such as actor Laurence Fishburne. In his third feature film, that high-profile performer played a supporting part in Coppola's master class of battle, and the director-actor collaboration returned to the battlefield a decade down the line thanks to *Garden of Stone* (1987).

From there, Fishburne led *The Tuskegee Airmen* (1995), a television film. But against all of his well-made war films, *Apocalypse Now* is the best of the bunch. Not even close, in full candor. Star actor Martin Sheen received common praise for his portrayal of Benjamin Willard, but at the beginning of that decade, he first showed up as a soldier by way of *Catch-22* (1970). Well after his collaboration with Coppola to end the 1970s, award-winning Martin Sheen played Robert E. Lee in *Gettysburg* (1993).

A few other war movies have featured Sheen throughout the years—he was the titular character in *The Execution of Private Slovik* (1974), for instance—but, again: *Apocalypse Now* is an all-time great of the medium, and easily Sheen's best wartime excursion. The same can be said for Robert Duvall, who previously played a major in the war-comedy *M*A*S*H* (1970).

He's a true master of genre, and the renown of *Apocalypse Now* nearly transcends Duvall's popularity in general. It laid the perfect landscape for more movie soldiers to traverse the battlefields in the following decade, with movies like *Platoon* (1985) cleaning up shop at the Oscar ceremonies. This was also a time for foreign films to get some shine, from *Das Boot* (1981) to *Come and See* (1985).

The nineties saw the release of the some of the genre's most lucrative films, from *The English Patient* (1996) to *Seven Years in Tibet* (1997). Of course, there's also *Saving Private Ryan* (1998), directed by Steven Spielberg. That world-famous creative genius is perhaps the greatest in the genre's history, and often times, he's considered among the best to ever do it. Much of that can be attributed to his contributions to war movies.

Of course, several actors throughout cinema have become associated with the genre, as well. For instance, take Tommy Lee Jones. He first appeared as a Master Sergeant in *Rolling Thunder* (1977), followed by a Captain in *Fire Birds* (1990). His first "Major" role in this regard was featured in *JFK* (1991), and then, he played a Gunnery Sergeant in *Heaven & Earth* (1993).

He followed up with another Major in *Blue Sky* (1994), and yet another in *Small Soldiers* (1998). Quite the array of serviceman, and in the twenty-first century, Tommy Lee continued appearing in several, high-quality war films. He played a Colonel in *Rules of Engagement* (2000), a Special Forces Trainer in *The Hunted* (2003), a Colonel in *Captain America: The First Avenger* (2011), a General in *Emperor* (2012), and a Marine in *The Burial* (2023).

That's an undeniably impressive resume, at least from a perspective of quantity. That said: some of Tommy Lee's war movies run the gamut of reception, whereas every film in which Cillian Murphy portrays a soldier proves to be of the utmost quality. He's outshined his contemporaries not just because of his output, nor the world-class caliber with which he performs, but also by virtue of the reverence that his respective titles have received.

There are even more modern war actors with whom Cillian has fought alongside that are well worth noting, such as Daniel Craig. After he worked with the Irishman at hand—more on their collaboration in a bit—Craig went on to star in *Defiance* (2008), directed by Edward Zwick. That's yet another filmmaker who's a hardened veteran of war movies, with titles such as *Glory* (1989) and *Courage Under Fire* (1995) being famous examples of the genre.

Another war movie soldier with whom Cillian has appeared is Robert Downey Jr., who first made waves on the battlefield thanks to *Tropic Thunder* (2008). Definitely more of a comedy than anything, but still a critical darling, and RDJ stole the show. It granted him grand levels of experience when he appeared with Cillian in another war movie much later down the line.

One year after *Tropic Thunder*, films like *Inglourious Basterds* (2009) and *The Hurt Locker* (2009) were surefire critical darlings, blockbuster successes that boast monumental name value. In that same twelve-month span, theaters saw the release of a few underrated war movies, too, such as *Brothers* (2009) and *The Messenger* (2009).

Already having established himself as a bona fide war movie hero, Woody Harrelson continued honing his prowess in *The Messenger* by Oren Moverman. In the following decade he appeared in *Midway* (2019), while before the current century, Harrelson co-starred in one of the greatest war movies ever made: *The Thin Red Line* (1998), written and directed by Terrence Malick. When accounting for *Welcome to Sarajevo* (1997), he's undoubtedly among the greatest actors to ever step foot on the battlefield.

Among the most famous actors of all time, Woody Harrelson isn't known for one particular genre. Not like George MacKay, an English actor who led the cast of *1917* (2019), and co-starred in *Private Peaceful* (2012). His war films aren't just master classes of storytelling—McKay consistently puts forth career-defining efforts whenever portraying a soldier. The first foray for McKay into battle was *Defiance*, which was released during the most booming period in the genre's rich history.

Around this time, plenty of actresses began appearing in numerous war movies, such as Mélanie Laurent. A performer from France, she made a name for herself around the world by leading *Inglourious Basterds*, the satirical depiction of World War II by American filmmaker Quentin Tarantino. She appeared with August Diehl, a German actor who's also put great work into the genre thanks to *Come What May* (2015), *Allied* (2016), *A Hidden Life* (2019), and *Munich – The Edge of War* (2022).

Through all those titles, *Inglourious Basterds* remains the best war film of August Diehl's career, and the same goes for Mélanie Lauren. But just one year after the release of that critical darling, Laurent starred in *The Round-Up* (2010), and even well before, she appeared in *Days of Glory* (2006). A pair of French films.

Those movies vary in popularity, but still. Three war movies in five years was historic for an actress, with only a select few like Meryl Streep standing out in history. In just her second on-screen appearance, Streep played a supporting part in *The Deer Hunter*, co-starring Robert De Niro and Christopher Walken.

All three of those talented thespians were recognized with nominations at the 51st Academy Awards: Best Actor for De Niro, Best Actress for Streep, and a Best Supporting Actor nom for Walken. The only winner among them Christopher Walken, who went onto appear in multiple, lesser-known war movies after the release of *The Deer Hunter*.

As for De Niro: Under the direction of Martin Scorsese, he played a veteran of the Vietnam War in *Taxi Driver* (1976). There are no combat scenes or battle preparations that can be found in the plot of *Taxi Driver*, but it may be the most famous film to ever explore the effects of post-traumatic stress disorder, and that's largely thanks to De Niro's efforts as the dynamic Travis Bickle.

Up next for De Niro was *The Deer Hunter*, but his output on the battlefield has waned ever since. He's added one more credit as a soldier thanks to *The Good Shepherd* (2006), in which he played a historical figure, General Bill Sullivan. That also marked his second stint behind the scenes as director, but again: *The Good Shepherd* is the last movie of prominence in which De Niro played a veteran. From there, he passed on the torch.

At the turn of the 2010s, one decade into the new millennium as a whole, the genre was at its peak. A few years after a historic 2009, one of the greatest periods for the genre, *American Sniper* (2014) became the highest-grossing war movie ever. Well, when adjusting for inflation, *Saving Private Ryan* (1998) was more successful. But in terms of gross, actual numbers accrued, *American Sniper* holds the record, raking in a whopping $547.4 million at the worldwide box office.

Based on Chris Kyle's autobiography of the same name—penned in 2012 with the help of both Scott McEwen and Jim DeFelice—the adaptation of *American Sniper* was written by Jason Hall. His efforts received widespread praise, with Hall even being nominated for Best Adapted Screenplay at the 87th Academy Awards. Also nominated was Bradley Cooper, in contention for Best Actor.

That renowned performer is also known for his famous portrayals of soldiers—aside Chris Kyle, the protagonist of *American Sniper*, he also played Templeton Peck in *The A-Team* (2010). A hero of the Vietnam War, that fictional soldier helps to render Cooper a recurring actor of the genre, even if *The A-Team* pales in comparison to the quality of *American Sniper*.

It was directed by Clint Eastwood, one of the most famous filmmakers in the medium's history, who had previously made war films such as *Flags of Our Fathers* and *Letters from Iwo Jima*, both of which were released in 2006. All three render him one of the genre's greatest directors, but that said: Eastwood is far from the only contemporary filmmaker to toil away on the set of a replica battlefield. From *Hacksaw Ridge* (2016) by Mel Gibson to *Da 5 Bloods* (2020) by Spike Lee, some of modern cinemas most popular all-time names have tried their hand at the war film.

Acting in numerous genre entries from *Gallipoli* (1981) and *Braveheart* (1995) to *The Patriot* (2000) and *We Were Soldiers* (2002), famous film figure Mel Gibson is among the best actors that war films have ever seen. He even holds auteur credits on *Braveheart*, with *Hacksaw Ridge* making him an essential director of the battlefield, as well.

As another example, refer to the career of British director Ken Loach. From *Land and Freedom* (1995) to *Route Irish* (2010), several of his films have been set against the backdrop of war, such as the United States invasion of Iraq that was initiated in 2003. In terms of Ken Loach's war films, neither *Land and Freedom* nor *Route Irish* boast much name value today. Not like the movie he made with Cillian Murphy as the lead.

After hitting mainstream success for his acclaimed efforts on *Kes* (1969), director Ken Loach went on to collaborate with some of the biggest names of the industry, and in the process, established himself as an all-time great. However, he's far from the only big-name director with whom Cillian has worked on a war film. The Irish actor has amassed a close collection of recurring collaborators ever since he made his debut as an actor—not on film, but with a stage play.

The Sons of Mr. Green Genes: Cillian's Early Years

Born in Cork, Ireland, on May 25, 1976, famous actor Cillian Murphy has put in tremendous work across various mediums as an actor since the turn of the twenty-first century. He's appeared in some of the most critically acclaimed and financially successful films of their respective decades—the same thing goes for television, albeit to a lesser extent.

Before winning the Academy Award for Best Actor thanks to his titular performance in *Oppenheimer* (2023), he was mostly known for his role as Thomas Shelby in a period drama series called *Peaky Blinders* (2013–2022). Hardcore film fans have long recognized his efforts, as he's collaborated multiple times with English filmmaker Christopher Nolan. What's more, Cillian has starred in two movies that were written by Alex Garland and directed by Danny Boyle, and on numerous occasions, he's appeared alongside such famous performers as Brendan Gleeson and Emily Blunt.

No matter their chosen craft, those are some well-known figures of the industry, and fans of Cillian's can likely name several movies on which he's worked with them each. Now with household name value, his movie roles are well-recognized by audiences around the world. However, little do some fans realize, Cillian actually began his career in entertainment by performing as a rock musician.

This was his first chosen craft, forming a love for music at a very young age. He was born to Brendan, who worked for the Department of Education, while Cillian's mother was employed as a French teacher. The oldest of four, Cillian has two younger sisters: Sile and Ora. With his younger brother Páidi, he even formed a rock band, called The Sons of Mr. Green Genes, after the song of the same name by guitarist Frank Zappa.

Although the two Murphy brothers were offered a deal with Acid Jazz Records, they eventually disbanded—Páidi was still in school, and Cillian's compositions were going to be taken by Acid Jazz for far less bang for their buck. Instead, Cillian turned his sights toward acting, and he's hardly looked back since.

He's continued his musical endeavors in various fashions throughout the years, but far and away, Cillian Murphy is most prominently known for his adeptness as an actor. He has enjoyed an eclectic career, as well, appearing in films of numerous kinds, and no matter the genre, almost every role under his belt has received widespread praise from critics. That said, there are a few types of films that seem to facilitate particularly poignant performances from the famous Irish thespian.

In spite of his recurring appearances under fan-favorite umbrellas such as horror and science fiction, Irish actor Cillian Murphy is at his best when on the battlefield. The war film he was first associated with was *The Wind That Shakes the Barley* (2006), which homes in on a pair of brothers from County Cork—where the film is shot, and where a majority of the Irish actors featured in the film are from. The brothers join the Irish Republican Army to fight against the United Kingdom for their country's independence. It's a famous plot, receiving widespread praise from critics and putting fans on notice regarding the prowess of Cillian Murphy.

That wasn't his first experience on the battlefield, though. In *The Trench* (1999) by William Boyd, he plays a soldier for the British amid the bloody battles of the First World War. Since, he's fought for both the Irish Army and the Czechoslovak Army, while also developing weapons for the United States of America. From *Cold Mountain* (2003) and *Anthropoid* (2016) to *Dunkirk* (2017) and *Oppenheimer* (2023), he's played a part in several depictions of famous real-life wars.

Four of his parts in war movies have been of the leading variety, while two were supporting and the other part was minor. But no matter the role, Cillian performs with a passion for peace, utilizing a powerful pair of iron lungs to chain-smoke cigarettes and deliver indelible dialogue. He's the greatest actor the genre's ever seen not just because of his volume of high-quality war movies, but also by dint of his skill, his prowess in front of a camera. Three of Cillian's best performances were given in the genre at hand—definitely not a coincidence.

There's a reason that dozens of high-profile thespians have made a name for themselves in the war genre throughout the history of Hollywood and beyond, as plenty of actors actually served in a prominent world conflict. Other times, they simply fit the part. Take Brad Pitt, for example. He's starred in some of the biggest war films ever made, such as *Inglourious Basterds* (2009).

That's a world-renowned entry of the genre, and thanks to others such *Seven Years in Tibet* (1997), *Troy* (2004), *Fury* (2014), and more, Brad Pitt is in turn one of the most prolific war actors ever to live. Of course, there's also Kirk Douglas, along with Marlon Brando, and frankly, those three names are only scratching the surface of actors who are known for appearing in high-quality war films.

More modern names include Willem Dafoe and Forest Whitaker, along with Sean Penn and Mark Wahlberg. There's also Denzel Washington, who first came into prominence as an actor in general thanks to his role as Private First Class Melvin Peterson in *A Soldier's Story* (1984). He then played Private Silas Trip in *Glory* (1989), followed by two roles in one year: Lt. Colonel Nathaniel Sterling in *Courage Under Fire* (1995), and a WWII veteran named Easy Rawlins in *Devil in a Blue Dress* (1995).

Against all of those worthy competitors—Pitt, Dafoe, Whitaker, Penn, Wahlberg, and Denzel, even – Cillian Murphy stands tall as the best, as cinema's greatest war hero. But before he ever made his on-screen debut, Cillian Murphy wiped the sweat from his brow by performing as characters in stage plays. Take *Disco Pigs* (1996–1998), for example.

A play by Enda Walsh, it would become somewhat prominent for Cillian later in his career. He didn't just appear in the feature-film adaptation, but also worked with his *Disco Pigs* co-star Orla Fitzgerald in a war film several years later. Even Enda Walsh—though not in the genre at hand, he would go on to collaborate with the playwright a couple of times down the line.

Although *The Tale of Sweety Barrett* has fallen even further into obscurity than it was upon release, it did mark Cillian's first time collaborating with Irish actor Brendan Gleeson. Over the next ten years, he'd work with Gleeson on four occasions, oftentimes in the most famous movies of their respective careers.

In 2020, Cillian spoke with *GQ* magazine about his most iconic characters. Detailing eight of his film characters—as well as Thomas Shelby from *Peaky Blinders*, the TV show—Cillian kicks off the interview by discussing his experience with *Disco Pigs*. He calls the adaptation the first role of his that "people took any notice of," and due to the play being his first official job as a professional actor, Cillian cites a great fondness for Darren as a character.

As for Cillian's other theatrical credits: He also appeared in *The Country Boy* (1999), along with *Juno and the Paycock* (1999). Another notable play in which he played a part was *Much Ado About Nothing* (1998), which was held at Kilkenny Castle. He played the character Claudio, a prominent part in the well-written plot of a comedy by William Shakespeare. But on top of these theatrical credits, Cillian also appeared in a few short films during his early years, starting with *Quando* in 1997.

Two years later, he played Brendan McBride in *Eviction* (1999), a short by Tom Waller, then portrayed "Grim Reaper Jr." in *At Death's Door* (1999). Neither of those is too prominent, though. Not like the feature *Sunburn* (1999). It remains highly underrated today, and not just because it features Cillian as the lead.

It's also a well-made movie in general, homing in on his protagonist Davin McDerby, a young Irish man who spends his summer in the United States. His co-stars included Ingeborga Dapkūnaitė, Barry Ward, and Sinead Keenan. Though by no means a well-known title today—nor was it popular upon release, even—*Sunburn* does remain prominent in the grand scheme of Cillian's career for marking his silver-screen debut.

Though primarily known as a dramatist, the first prowess of Cillian's on display was actually of the comedic ilk. Punctuated by the din of a nearby store alarm, *Sunburn* begins with Cillian's protagonist Davin running down the sidewalk of an idle city street. Clearly, he just stole something. Turning a corner—physically, not spiritually just yet—David hides behind a doorway, stashes the loot in his pocket, and proceeds about his day.

He needed the money for an abortion, and he retrieved it through painstaking means only to discover that the woman he impregnated has decided to keep the baby. What does Davin do? He leaves the country, of course. Though the lead is hard to root for at times, it's nonetheless a well-written script with endearing characters across the board. Memorable plot points, as well, and thanks to a strict adherence to story structure, it's also perfectly paced.

Since that comedy-drama by Nelson Hume, he's shifted his sights to cinema and hardly ever looked back. The few exceptions include his stints on television, some music videos, and even a couple of video games. A theater actor at heart, he also appeared in a few other stage plays after leading the cast of *Sunburn*—just one example is *The Seagull* (2002), by dramatist Anton Chekhov.

This wide array of credits showcases his ongoing commitment to the craft, spreading his prowess across various mediums aside from film and television. But if one were to hold a gun to his head in an act of interrogation and ask his preferred outlet of performing, the greatest war actor to ever live would undoubtedly cite the cinema.

Amid a hot streak of war films produced in Hollywood and beyond, one flew a bit too far beneath the radar of prominence.

It's called *The Trench*, written and directed by William Boyd. And although it wasn't released internationally, the movie was rather overshadowed by some of the biggest war movies of the decade—take *Three Kings* (1999), for instance.

Written and directed by David O. Russell, it was released in America just two weeks after the war film by Boyd. Receiving acclaim from critics around the world and making admirable money in theaters, *Three Kings* was much more prominent in the overall landscape of cinema. Other war films, too—although they came out in the previous year, titles like *The Thin Red Line* (1998) and *Saving Private Ryan* have drowned out the resonance of Billy Boyd's adventure.

Though not the best film from anyone involved—or even the best war movie, as plenty members of the cast would work in the genre again—*The Trench* features impressive efforts from everyone involved. From the perspective of technical filmmaking, like camerawork and sound design, it's also highly underrated.

One Man's Meat: Cillian's First Deployment

Nearing the close of 1915, a year-and-a-half into the grueling battles of World War I, the Allies are backed into a proverbial corner as the Germans are still well in control of their territories. With the help of their British contemporaries, the French army thus plans an offensive that will launch over the summer as a battle on the Western Front—specifically, in northern France, around the narrow and murky waters of the infamous river Somme.

Setting out with their closest European allies, the British army partook in one of the bloodiest battles in the history of humanity. For more than four months in 1916—from July 1 to November 18, the midpoint of World War I, when the violence was at its peak—the Anglo-French forces fought off the invading German army at the historic Somme river, located in Picardy, France. That notorious body of water was home to more than a million casualties across both sides of the conflict, just 20,000 in a single day, with those numbers resulting in a milestone of bloodshed that's forever cemented in history.

In the middle of the battle, on August 21, a British documentary of propagandic proportions shined light on the Expeditionary Forces of Britain as they prepared for the Battle of the Somme. Appropriately called The Battle of the Somme, the film goes on to depict the first few days of battle, with footage that includes various elements of warfare from trench fighting to medical situations.

The documentary was highly successful, accruing more than 20 million viewers during its initial showing, its first month and a half on the market. It was a historic release, not just because of the numbers it amassed in viewership, but also because of the camera techniques that were used by Geoffrey Malins and J.B. McDowell to properly showcase the War in a realistic way.

A popular, black-and-white silent film—rescreened in 2006 after a process of restoration—*The Battle of the Somme* documentary paved the way for many other impressions of the most devastating conflict of World War I. Take a look at *The Trench*, for example, which marked the directorial debut of Scottish author William Boyd.

PROLOGUE TO THE TRENCH

In the high summer of 1916, in northern France, the British Army prepared for the biggest offensive of the First World War. As hundreds of thousands of troops massed in the rear, waiting for the order to attack, a reduced force was put in place to hold the front-line trenches.

The first war film of Cillian's career was his third credit overall, a relatively unknown title starring Paul Nicholls and Daniel Craig. It's called *The Trench*, written and directed by William Boyd, and it homes in on a squadron of British soldiers in 1916 as they make their preparations for the Battle of the Somme. If only they knew for what they were truly in store.

In a supporting role, Cillian shows up as Pte. Rag Rookwood, and he can be seen as early as the opening sequence while playing cards with a fellow soldier. In fact, the movie's first line is delivered by Rookwood, who goes on to bond with his other platoon brothers over one of their collections of softcore pornography, and a few moments later, the soldiers stand up straight and answer to Sgt. Telford Winter, who's played by Daniel Craig.

Several years before he cemented his status as a household name of cinema—thanks to leading roles in *Layer Cake* (2004) and *Casino Royale* (2006)—that famous actor performed brilliantly as the sergeant of this platoon. Speaking of *Casino Royale*: A literary character created by Ian Fleming, protagonist James Bond, is also a war veteran, having risen to the rank of Commander before the Second World War met its long-awaited end. Just like Cillian, the depiction of the Somme by director Billy Boyd helped to hone Craig's skills at portraying a soldier of war.

Oddly enough, Billy Boyd would go on to write an entry in the *James Bond* series of fiction novels. It was announced by Ian Fleming's estate in 2012 that Billy would pen the piece, and one year later, the book was released in the United Kingdom under the title of *Solo*. This sequel wouldn't be adapted into a live-action movie with Craig, or anything, but still. The continuation novel of the character that Craig is most commonly associated with gave Billy an even greater association with soldiers.

From a contemporary perspective, Daniel Craig's efforts in *The Trench* should be held in much higher regard, and to be frank, the same thing goes for every member among the cast of this highly underrated war film. Paul Nicholls portrays the protagonist, named Private Billy McFarlane, while Danny Dwyer plays a supporting part as Lance Corporal Victor Dell. Those are two famous performers, particularly the latter, and just like Craig as their sergeant, they fire on all cylinders as a pair of youthful British soldiers. That's not all, though.

Other actors among the cast include the talented James D'Arcy, along with the wonderful Ben Whishaw—the latter making his on-screen debut, to boot. Some significant name value, even if most of these actors were just starting out. Although they weren't superstars at the time that *The Trench* was released, the world-class talent of the all-star cast is clear-cut when revisiting the project itself.

Once their characters are introduced and the exposition is established, *The Trench* kicks into third gear as the Battle of the Somme shifts to first. After receiving word that plans have been put on hold to move forward with the offensive, the regiment posts up in a trench and await further command. Anxiety soon arises, creating some intimate insight into the subtleties of battle.

These aren't the travails that are typically touched on in the overall landscape of war films. Standing around in tedium, the soldiers in *The Trench* are essentially waiting to be attacked, exchanging lines of well-written dialogue in lieu of firing their weapons. But after one of the soldiers looks out of a loophole of the eponymous location, a gunshot ricochets and pierces him in the head.

This is the plot's inciting incident, and it only expands from there. It's a poignant story, and the primary characters establish meaningful dynamics while delivering indelible dialogue. They banter back and forth while waiting in the wings, but to punctuate the humor that arises from their exchanges, Sgt. Winter resurfaces and keeps his soldiers in check. The film is well-paced until the poignancy of its ending.

A technical triumph, *The Trench* excels across the board of behind-the-scenes filmmaking, as well. By itself, the cinematography makes the movie worth a watch, with engaging shot value and careful camera movements. Thought-out tactics of blocking, as well. The specific spots in which the soldiers stand, the careful manners in which they traverse the passages of the trench—in many ways, the location is rendered a character in itself by dint of keen direction by Boyd.

You'll become acquainted with its corridors and attached to the soldiers that reside therein—not individually, but as a whole. There are too many faces, names, and uniforms in *The Trench* for everyone to fully develop as characters. All that said: The ultimate fate of Cillian's character Pte. Rag Rookwood will reverberate with audiences forever. His first war movie, *The Trench* also marks the first time in which a soldier played by Cillian suffers a brutal and prominent death.

Soldiers in the trenches of the First World War travailed through just as many hardships in their base as they did outside on the battlefield. Famine, disease, oncoming attacks—the trenches were great lines of defense from heavy degrees of artillery, and they facilitate surprise attacks by digging underneath, but around every corner of those infamous, muddy hell holes, death consumed the combatants who entrusted the base with their lives.

The trenches of the battlefield throughout World War I became something of a home for the soldiers. Intense action was punctuated by long stints of tedium, with downtime usually being occupied by idle chit-chat, stories of home, and mindless games. Pictures of naked ladies, and the like. But the overarching threat of death was looming around every conversation and through every crumbling tunnel, creating a palpable suspense for the soldiers and their every waking moment.

For centuries, soldiers had been utilizing the defensive tactics of trenches for various means during warfare. Since the Battle of Dara in 530 CE—when Roman general Belisarius ordered his legion to create a trench, granted, to no avail—this has been an ongoing technique, all throughout the Middle Ages and into a modern setting. The paradigm of attack was typically unsuccessful, as waves of soldiers with poised bayonets would emerge out of the trench and charge straight into no man's land.

Not the most effective of tactics, but by the time the Great War rolled around, artillery weapons had become so advanced that the purpose of trench warfare itself saw some dramatic developments. That worked both ways, not just when considering the methods of attack available from the trench, but also the lines of defense that hold up there from.

Heavy artillery would bombard the British trenches for days at a time, with other weapons such as poison gas being deployed from the Germans, as well. Death by sniper rifle was also rife within the trenches, as soldiers surveying the battlefield (typically with periscopes) would get picked off one by one. A lot to keep track of—for as much downtime as the soldiers had within the trenches of World War I, there wasn't much sleep going on.

In tandem with the unsettling prospect of death, the general conditions of the trenches were less than satisfactory, contributing greatly to the men's dearth of rest. Rats were rife, first of all. That'll keep anyone on their toes, let alone awake. But frankly, having rodents as their bunkmates ranked as one of the least of their worries—the dangers from within the trenches paled in lethal comparison to the destructive nature of Germany's weapons.

No matter how aware of their surroundings a given soldier may have been, death within the trench would come when they'd least expect it. Take Rag Rookwood, for instance. In Billy Boyd's brutal and bloody depiction of battle, Cillian's character gets blown to bits. For whatever reason, his characters are consistently killed off in his war films, and in memorable fashion to boot.

Here in *The Trench*, his demise materializes at the midpoint and turns the plot on its head. Found by protagonist Billy McFarlane as he rounds a corner of the trench, the body of Cillian's character is lying dead in the dirt, his arms sprawled out and decorated with blood. Here's the thing, though: Merely half of his body remains—specifically, the torso.

Brutal stuff, and of course, you won't see much of Cillian from there. Even before then, his lines of dialogue were few and far between. But the careful craft of acting by no means revolves solely around the constant exchanging of words—it's also about the expressions of the face, the ability of someone to seamlessly bend those expressions into their physical will. Cillian has that in spades, and across the board, the cast is on par with his perfection.

At the behest of the director, each of the primary actors spent a night in a makeshift trench, replicating the distress of the British Army soldiers to whom they respectfully pay homage. This undoubtedly played a part in the realism of the film, with *The Trench* boasting a gritty atmosphere around every corner of production. With some exceptions, it's a historically accurate depiction of war to boot, with the authenticity being primarily attributed to the commitment of William Boyd.

Two of the director's family members served in World War I: his grandfather, and his great uncle. They were both injured, as well—the former at Passchendaele, and the latter in the Somme. He has many ties to the war, and he did it great justice with *The Trench*. This is among the finest works of Boyd's career, and his only feature film to date.

He's primarily known as a novelist. However, he's made other contributions to cinema, penning the scripts for such movies as *Stars and Bars* (1988), *Mister Johnson* (1990), *Tune in Tomorrow* (1990), and *A Good Man in Africa* (1994). Hardly any of those hold prominence from a contemporary perspective, but then again, neither does *The Trench*.

Perhaps the most lauded script of William Boyd's career came with a co-credit on *Chaplin* (1992), a highly acclaimed film by director Richard Attenborough. In the twenty-first century, after the release of his well-made war film, Boyd landed another co-writing credit on a historical drama titled *Man to Man* (2005). Through all of that work he's put into the medium, *The Trench* is without a doubt his greatest contribution. But he isn't the only creative who excels from behind the scenes.

While sitting in the editing room, Jim Clark pieced the project together with well-timed tactics of continuity transitioning. Before working on *The Trench*, he directed several films such as *Every Home Should Have One* (1970), *Rentadick* (1972), and *Madhouse* (1974). Those may not ring any bells, but his previous credits as an editor are highly regarded today.

He collaborated multiple times with legendary film director John Schlesinger, editing such famous films as *Darling* (1965), *Midnight Cowboy* (1969), *The Day of the Locust* (1975), and *Marathon Man* (1976). Four critical darlings that feature essential efforts from the editor, with Jim Clark putting those same skills on display in *The Trench* by William Boyd.

This is among the finest war films of its decade in spite of some lackluster numbers of success. Given its reception, *The Trench* should also be considered one of the genre's most underrated movies—not just of the nineties, but throughout cinema as a whole. While its documentary counterpart *The Battle of the Bulge* was seen by audiences everywhere back in 1916, this fictional story was by no means a success upon release. Just look at the meager money it made in movie theaters, for instance.

Although there aren't hard-hitting numbers in that regard available to the public, there are some numbers of success out there that help identify its quality. Daniel Craig's performance was lauded across the board, with the thespian being nominated for Best Actor at the British Independent Spirit Awards. If his character had stuck around a bit longer to shave his face and smoke his cigarettes, Cillian could've been in contention regarding Best Supporting Actor.

Alas, Craig's nomination is evident enough of the caliber of these performances, even if that famous British actor ultimately came up short. What's more is that, as a whole, *The Trench* was nominated at the same ceremony as Craig in the category of Best Achievement in Production, and justifiably so. Granted, in terms of the breadth of its budget, *The Trench* is just what the aforementioned ceremony implies: an independent film. Don't go in expecting large-scale battles, or anything.

There's a fair amount of gunplay in the film's climactic sequence, but mostly, *The Trench* is an exercise in atmospheric storytelling. For that, Billy Boyd and his team were revered thanks to the set that they created, but even then, critics were rather harsh in their reviews as a whole. In hindsight, they weren't in the wrong when offering complaints about the pacing. But for the performances of its cast alone, not to mention the production value for a film of this degree, it without a doubt stands the brutal test of time.

As explosions resound in the distance and soldiers shout through the trench, Cillian experiences the travails of war in just the second film of his career. Upon release, *The Trench* deserved far more praise, and if anything, its name value has only waned throughout the years. Here's hoping it claims the status of cult classic at some point down the line.

One title that was (at least at one point) widely recognized as a high-quality tale is *Juno and the Paycock*, a play by Irish dramatist Seán O'Casey. He's one of the most famous playwrights to ever live, and along with the likes of Samuel Beckett with World War II, he's an Irishman who's often associated with a certain series of conflicts.

A Principle's a Principle: Playing a Veteran in a Stage Play

In the same year as his first on-screen deployment, Cillian played a part in a stage play called *Juno and the Paycock* (1999), directed by Gary Hines. It's the second of the *Dublin Trilogy* by Irish playwright Seán O'Casey, succeeding *The Shadow of a Gunman* and preceding *The Plough and the Stars*. All three pieces were highly revered, remaining the best plays of O'Casey's oeuvre—in particular, the first two.

This was Cillian's first play of true prominence as, sure, *Disco Pigs* by Enda Walsh helped to put him on the map. But that was an original production, whereas *Juno and the Paycock* with Cillian was produced by Gary Hines from an original writing by O'Casey, one that's widely regarded among the greatest plays of the twentieth century, and even of all time. It's part of a spiritual trilogy—not connected by characters or plot points, but rather by themes and setting—with the first entry *The Shadow of a Gunman* premiering in 1923 at the Abbey Theatre in Dublin.

First opening to the public in 1904, the Abbey Theatre was the home of other Irish playwrights of the highest profiles, such as Lady Gregory and William Butler Yeats. Each entry of O'Casey's trilogy premiered at the Abbey, with the first play being set during the Irish War of Independence. Through both well-implemented subtext and overtly humorous plot points, each entry in the trilogy homes in on the struggles of citizen life brought about by the brutalities of battle.

The War for Irish Independence (1919–1921) was in many respects unconventional, as the IRA (Irish Republican Army) was largely composed of bricklayers and butchers, stonemasons and shoemakers—the artisans, in essence. They were the working class, a guerrilla army who became known as "Sinn Féin Volunteers" after a political party that's rooted primarily in republicanism.

These volunteers are also known as Die-hards, which they're often called in *Juno and the Paycock*, the second entry in O'Casey's trilogy and the one that was staged with Cillian Murphy. He played a prominent part as Johnny, a veteran in Ireland's War of Independence who lost his arm during battle, and was even shot in the hip amid the infamous Easter Rising.

```
Johnny appears at the door on the left. He
can be plainly seen now; he is a thin, del-
icate fellow, somewhat younger than Mary.
He has evidently gone through a rough
time. His face is pale and drawn; there
is a tremulous look of indefinite fear in
his eyes. The left sleeve of his coat is
empty, and he walks with a slight halt.
```

Off the bat, the tragedies of war that have been inflicted on Johnny are evident in his demeanor. Hardly any dialogue has been delivered to or from the character, and he's already made a significant impact on the story re: his contributions to a pair of prominent conflicts in which he fought bravely for his country.

Taking place when World War II had yet to reach its peak, the Easter Rising was the setting for *The Plough and the Stars*, the final entry in the *Dublin Trilogy* by playwright Seán O'Casey. He worked out of real-life continuity, with the Easter Rising being the fons et origo of the subsequent Irish conflicts: Just before Austria-Hungary declared war on Serbia, insurgence across the continent was rearing its head in Ireland.

A revolutionary period had long been brewing due to Britain's control of the country, resulting in several armed conflicts between compatriots who just couldn't see eye to eye. Protestant loyalists supported British regulation, while the Irish nationalists were in direct opposition, desperately seeking independence and thus creating a republic.

In April of 1916, these tensions came to what seemed to be a crescendo, as nationalists of Ireland stormed their poverty-stricken capital and waged war on British reinforcements. Artillery shells and gunfire rained down on the rebels for five days consecutively, which resulted in the death of 260 citizens. They took a heavier toll than the rebels themselves, who suffered around 80 casualties at the hands of the British forces.

Though the necessity of those lengths have been debated by historians, there's no denying the futility of the following events. More than 3,500 citizens were arrested, and thrown into the confines of Kilmainham Gaol prison. Most were released within the subsequent month of May, but while they were kept behind bars, fourteen so-called ringleaders of the infamous insurrection were led to an internal courtyard and executed by firing squad.

This led to further hostilities from the IRA, with the War of Independence commencing just three years after the Easter-week rebellion. It's the setting for *The Shadow of a Gunman*, and the conflict that caused Johnny Boyle from *Juno and the Paycock* to lose his primary limb. His afflictions are a constant source of discussion, like a capillary wave that's traveling along the surface of the tea that's being served by his beloved mother Juno.

She's one half of the eponymous couple—her nickname being Juno thanks to the primitive experiences of her life always taking place in June—while her husband "Captain Jack" is referred to as a peacock. At least, that's what he's called by his wife, on numerous occasions and often with resentment.

```
Mrs Boyle:   Isn't he come in yet?
Mary:        No, mother.
Mrs Boyle:   Oh,  he'll  come  in  when  he
likes;  struttin'  about  the  town  like  a
paycock with Joxer, I suppose.
```

In lieu of keeping a steady job, Captain Jack struts around town with his best friend Joxer Daly. The two frequent pubs when they should be seeking employment, and with regard to Captain Jack: he feigns a pain in his legs, and on top of never working, he's rarely ever home. This leaves his wife to pick up the pieces in the unsteady tenements of Ireland's capital city, managing their house and caring for their children—the beleaguered second born, Johnny is the younger brother of Mary, who's currently on strike. Something the playwright can relate to.

A laborer himself, O'Casey worked on the Great Northern Railway for nine years as his first major source of income. It's then he was exposed to the harsh conditions brought about by labor bosses, leading to a newfound interest in the prospect of Irish nationalism. After meeting Jim Larkin—founder of the Irish Transport and General Workers Union—the playwright became greatly invested in the roots of his culture and eventually Gaelicizing his name, which was previously John Casey. He even familiarized himself with a woodwind instrument called uillean pipes, also known as bagpipes, and read up on the works of the important literary figures from Ireland's glowing past.

Intensely studying the intricacies of his fellow Irishmen's intellectual activity, O'Casey parlayed his knowledge into writing ballads. By the time he transitioned to playwriting, he had already been elected as General Secretary of the Irish Citizen Army—again, established by Larkin—and even stepped down from the position. He'd completely shifted his sights to playwriting, but still imbedded his new line of work with his well-known passions for politics.

In *Juno and the Paycock*, he paints his characters with the colors of Ireland's working-class tenements, and shines light on the effects that Larkin's war had on the everyday people of the country they so desperately sought to protect. The personalities in *Juno* create an everlasting dynamic that resonated fondly with audiences, though not so much with critics, who bore a bit of resentment for O'Casey due to his innate propensity for storytelling. He spent his life working, not attending school. The playwright didn't even learn how to read until the age of twelve.

Now, his pieces are held in the highest of regards, not just in Ireland, but around the world. After premiering in 1924, the play has been adapted to various mediums such as film, television, and even radio. Of course, many theater directors have gone on to lead the play, as well. Take Garry Hynes, for instance. She directed Cillian in *Juno and the Paycock* one year after solidifying a spot in the history books for winning the highly coveted Tony.

For her management over *The Beauty Queen of Leanne*—written by Martin McDonough in 1996—she won the Tony Award for Direction and thus became the award's first female recipient. For the most part, her production of O'Casey's seminal war-torn *Juno* was also well-received, and that's partly thanks to the efforts of its cast. On top of Cillian, there's also Michael Gambon, who shows up as Johnny's father: the strutting Captain Jack.

Although the production by Hynes is unavailable to view online, there are still a few reviews that are floating around on the internet. Writing for *The Irish Times*, critic Derek West noted that Cillian's effort, "captures the terror and the self-immolation of Johnny's egotism," and praised the production as a whole for its close adherence to the source material.

Director Garry Hynes also put her spin on *The Plough and the Stars*, albeit sans a role for Cillian, and nearly a century after the original plays were put together, Hynes returned to the *Dublin trilogy* to deliver DruidO'Casey, a sprawling theatrical epic that combined all three plays into a single six-hour production.

A revered theater company, Druid had previously put on productions of this proportion with other playwrights such as Shakespeare. Hynes even made DruidSynge several years prior, but with DruidO'Casey, everyone involved received widespread praise, further showcasing Garry's understanding of the source material and the quality of her collaboration with Cillian.

In the same year as their work on *Juno and the Paycock*, the two teamed up for another stage play, called *The Country Boy*, and in the twenty-first century, they collaborated once again with *The Playboy of the Western World* (2005). Originally written by John Millington Synge, it featured Cillian in the primary role. His character wasn't a soldier, though.

The famous *Juno and the Paycock* marked the only instance in which Cillian portrayed a soldier—or, in this case, a veteran—on stage. Since transitioning to the silver screen at the turn of the century, however, Cillian has added several more film roles to his roster of war characters that solidify his claim as the greatest.

A wide-ranging actor, Cillian has amassed numerous roles throughout the years that have resonated fondly with film buffs even decades after the respective movie's release. One example is *28 Days Later* (2002), directed by Danny Boyle from a script by Alex Garland. It was revered when it was released in theaters, and in a contemporary light, the fans have held it in equally high regard—not just *28 Days Later*, but also the efforts of Cillian Murphy as the survivor of a zombie apocalypse.

Before returning to the war genre, he took a bit of a break, starting with three films in the same year: *On the Edge* (2001), *How Harry Became a Tree* (2001), and *Disco Pigs* (2001). The last of those three is relevant for being an adaptation of Enda Walsh's play of the same name, in which Cillian also starred. Now directed by Kristen Sheridan, the film saw less success upon release than its original counterpart.

But Cillian's efforts were widely praised, and justifiably so. There is another credit of those from 2001 worth homing in on: *On the Edge*, which marked his first time working with actor Stephen Rea. The two would become close collaborators, appearing in numerous productions with one another, and *On the Edge* by John Carney is still among their best.

Then came the most prominent movie up to that point in Cillian's career: *28 Days Later*. He plays the protagonist, a bicycle courier named Jim, and he performs to perfection every pedal of the way. Aside from war, this is the genre that's most often associated with the career of Cillian Murphy, and given the quality of the zombie movie at hand, it's easy to see why. Among the finest horror films ever made—let alone of the twenty-first century—*28 Days Later* received widespread praise from pundits of the industry.

It isn't just a famous zombie film that was popular among fans—*28 Days Later* is also a technically efficient horror movie that influenced filmmakers everywhere. It sparked a resurgence of the zombie subgenre, and it ranks among the finest films thereof. It may just be the best—for what it's worth, though, Boyle has gone on record saying he doesn't consider it one at all. But for the most part, audiences agree that it undoubtedly fits the bill.

Several decades prior, in true auteur fashion, George A. Romero wrote, directed, shot, and edited the classic *Night of the Living Dead* (1968). Quite the acclaimed film, and it gives *28 Days Later* a solid run for its money. Even Romero's sequel, *Dawn of the Dead* (1978) from a decade down the line—often cited as one of the best. Less popular but still revered titles include *Braindead* (1992), followed by *Resident Evil* (2002) in the same year as Danny Boyle's masterpiece.

Speaking of: On a couple of occasions, Boyle has cited the original *Resident Evil* video game—on which the films of the same name are directly based—from 1996 as a direct source of influence for *28 Days Later*. In turn, Boyle's endeavor went on to inspire dozens of other titles in the video game medium, such as *The Last of Us* (2013) by Naughty Dog.

What's more is that, after the success of *28 Days*, several other zombie films materialized in the mainstream. First was *Dawn of the Dead*, a reboot by Zack Snyder that was released in 2004, along with Edgar Wright's spoof called *Shaun of the Dead*, which premiered that same year. With regard to the latter, it helped films like *Zombieland* (2009) coin what's known as a zombie comedy—or, a zom com, if you will. Those are two of the funniest films from the 2000s, and their respective creators were inspired by *28 Days Later*.

The primary source of inspiration stemming from the overflowing fountain of *28 Days Later* can be traced to the nature of its zombies. With Danny Boyle and Alex Garland to thank, the antagonists changed the game of the apocalyptic subgenre by harboring legitimate speed. These creatures could actually run, in other words, providing fans with far more horrifying moments than are typically featured in the plodding nature of zombie movies past.

Video games, comic books, television—the impact of *28 Days Later* spreads far beyond the silver screens of the cinema, with authors like Max Brooks and comic book artists such as Robert Kirkman also giving the movie its flowers of inspiration. Of course, the movie spawned a massive franchise, as well, featuring film sequels, comic book spinoffs, and more.

This wasn't a blockbuster, award-winning success, or anything. For the most part, the fame of *28 Days Later* was accrued after its release. In hindsight, Cillian receives all the credit in the world by film fans for his indelible performance as Jim. Channeling a certain grit and intensity – both on full display in his demeanor whenever he appears on screen – he led his first horror project to absolute greatness, with *28 Days Later* being widely recognized from a contemporary perspective as one of the greatest horror movies ever.

Casting director Gail Stevens suggested to Danny Boyle, director of *28 Days Later*, that he give an audition to Cillian and consider him for the lead. After watching *Disco Pigs*, the casting director was impressed with Cillian's caliber, and justifiably so. Though not many audiences are familiar with *Disco Pigs*, the seminal modern zombie movie with Cillian as the lead is widely recognized today as one of the subgenre's all-time greats. He's frequently associated with

28 Days Later, and when considering the power of his performance in tandem with the quality of the film itself, it's easy to see why.

Against an $8 million budget, it made $84.6 million in ticket sales. Given its success, fans saw a franchise coming, and *28 Weeks Later* lived up to the hype in many of their eyes. While it certainly pales in comparison to its predecessor—they should've hired Cillian again, though it's worth noting he was busy with another project—the sequel nonetheless utilizes a talented cast (Jeremy Renner and Rose Byrne, for instance) to see a well-written script come into engaging fruition.

During the COVID-19 pandemic—which brought many parallels to the surface of the plot of the film itself—*28 Days Later* saw something of a resurgence in online viewership. That said, soon thereafter, it actually became impossible to watch. Unless you had a physical copy, that is, and if you do, hold on tight like it's a firearm in battle.

Its paucity of availability with regard to digital streaming services can be directly attributed to some issues with licensing. Though the sequel *28 Weeks Later* can still be found online, the original is nowhere to be found, lost in the void of the apocalyptic wasteland in which the plot of the film is set. All that said: The rights to *28 Days Later* have been bought back by producer Andrew MacDonald, who then traded the property to Sony Pictures and solidified the deal of another, sought-after sequel.

Fans have recently been anticipating yet another entry in the series, as three of the primary creatives of the first film are in talks to return. Both Danny Boyle and Alex Garland have stated that the script is speculatively titled "28 Years Later," which sounds about right, and get this: On numerous occasions, Cillian has confirmed his reprisal as Jim in the upcoming sequel of the world-famous franchise.

That'd be quite the sight for a couple of reasons, one being that, since the release of *28 Days Later*, he added a recurring character to his eclectic roster of film roles—the image of that infamous super-villain likely popped into your head off the bat, and the Batman movies will of course be touched on in a bit. But he's proven capable of tackling a character numerous times, and what's more is that he's also revisited the apocalyptic subgenre. At this point, it only makes sense for Cillian to return, especially if Danny and Alex are speculated to join.

They're two of the names most often associated with Cillian's career in cinema. At this point, it's Brendan Gleeson, Emily Blunt, and Christopher Nolan, along with the one-two-punch of Danny and Alex. After the release of *28 Days Later*, the trio would reunite on a sci-fi thriller called *Sunshine* (2007)—in the twentieth century, however, director Danny Boyle was primarily known for his work with Ewan McGregor.

They collaborated on *Shallow Grave* (1994)—the first film credit for Boyle and the second for McGregor—followed by *Trainspotting* (1996), their most popular, as well as *A Life Less Ordinary* (1997). Though not quite as prolific, Cillian is one of Boyle's closest collaborators, as well. As for Alex Garland: He debuted as a screenwriter with *28 Days*, then went on to direct *Ex Machina* (2015), *Annihilation* (2018), and *Men* (2022) to great acclaim. Even all these years later—for both Danny and for Alex—one of their all-time greatest works is *28 Days Later*.

When giving his *GQ* magazine interview, Cillian cited *Shallow Grave* and *Trainspotting* as some of the most inspirational movies he'd seen growing up. He considered it an honor to work with Danny Boyle, who in turn gave Cillian the perfect canvas for the latter to pain his masterpiece. At least, that's what *28 Days Later* was for Cillian back when it was released.

At the first official ceremony of the Irish Film & Television Awards, the actor of the hour was in the running for Best Actor in a Leading Role – Film. His first nomination of many in that regard, as the IFTA as a whole would become the greatest champion of Cillian Murphy, awarding him numerous honors for his work in both cinema and television.

He lost the nomination to Andrew Scott in *Dead Bodies* (2003), while other runners-up for Best Actor included Michael McElhatton for *Spin the Bottle* (2003), Aidan Quinn in *Song for a Raggy Boy* (2003), as well as Colin Farrell for *SWAT* (2003). Like Cillian, they all put forth admirable performances that could've been victorious in any other setting. No matter, though. Over the following few years, Cillian would stake his claim as one of Ireland's greatest actors by dint of several famous film characters.

After his breakthrough success in the fan-favorite realm of horror, Cillian appeared in a film called *Intermission* (2003), then *Girl with a Pearl Earring* (2003). They were both praised across the board of reception, and they both feature Cillian in notable roles. In the former, Colin Farrell stars as Lehiff, with that countryman of Cillian's actually having debuted in a war movie that's known as *Frankie Starlight* (1995).

At the century's turn, Farrell led the cast of *Tigerland* (2000) to relative acclaim, playing Private Roland Buzz during the Vietnam War. Just a couple of years thereafter, Farrell co-starred in *Hart's War* (2002). Quite the output—within his first six credits on the silver screens of cinema, Colin Farrell collected three war movies in total.

Combat zones seemed to be a preferred setting throughout his career's earlier phases, which is also when he appeared alongside Cillian Murphy. With regard to *Pearl Earring*: the general of war movies acts alongside Colin Firth, whose cinematic military service should be held in high regard.

He appeared with Nicole Kidman as a prisoner of war in *The Railway Man* (2013), and in that same decade, Firth played a general in *1917* (2019). When accounting for his role in *The English Patient* (1996) and an Oscar-winning effort in *The King's Speech* (2010), he's without a doubt in consideration as cinema's greatest soldier. As it just so happens, he appeared alongside the general himself in *Girl with a Pearl Earring*.

It also marked the first collaboration between Cillian and Tom Wilkinson, with the latter having portrayed two soldiers just a few credits prior to *Pearl Earring*. In *Molokai: The Story of Father Damien* (1999), he portrayed Joseph Dutton, a lieutenant of the Union Army, and just a few months later, Wilkinson showed up in *The Patriot* (2000) as General Lord Cornwallis. Famous names, though that particular actor doesn't boast anywhere near the number of credits as his contemporary from Ireland.

In his next stint as a marksman on the battlefield, Cillian's appearance is actually rather brief, but he kills it in the soldier archetype and helps his celebrated co-stars bring a poignant scene to life. The movie is called *Cold Mountain* (2003), and it holds up wonderfully with hindsight. Not that it was condemned by critics upon release, or anything like that. It was held in high regard, evident by its sundry numbers of success. But now, *Cold Mountain* holds up as especially relevant for featuring Cillian as a soldier.

He Hasn't Eaten in Days: Appearing in a Period War Drama

With Anthony Minghella as the auteur, *Cold Mountain* is based on the novel of the same name, written by Charles Frazier in 1997. They follow the same story, set at the end of the American Civil War as an injured soldier of the Confederate army—named William "W.P." Inman, and played by Jude Law in Minghella's adaptation—deserts his regime and travels home to reconvene with the love of his life. Her name is Ada, played by Nicole Kidman, and while Inman is away at war, she faces travails of her own, unable to keep her farm running properly. It's a good thing he's coming home, as she needs him now more than ever.

A compelling plot, thanks entirely to the efforts of the author of the novel on which the film is based. The recipient of the National Book Award for Fiction, author Charles Frazier beat such juggernauts of the medium as Ward Just and Don DeLillo for the highly coveted literary accolade. With *Thirteen Moons* (2006), also set during the American Civil War and receiving acclaim from critics, Frazier released a brilliant follow up to his debut novel *Cold Mountain*. But without a doubt, the latter represents the peak of Frazier's oeuvre.

As for the movie: Minghella's vision is seen into praiseworthy fruition by one of the greatest casts ever assembled. On top of Law and Kidman, there's also Renée Zellweger, as well as Eileen Atkins. But those are just a few of the names, with others including Brendan Gleeson and Philip Seymour Hoffman. Some famous performers, and even then, that's still hardly scratching the surface of this star-studded affair. Performers from around the world were gathered to compile the cast, with other names including Natalie Portman, Donald Sutherland, Giovanni Ribisi, and Ray Winstone. Quite the array of actors.

Of course, there's also Cillian Murphy, who plays a minor character named Bardolph. In spite of the brief nature of his appearance, the soldier played by Cillian is entirely memorable thanks to the work of the Irish actor. No matter the given amount of screen time, everyone's performances are top tier in *Cold Mountain*, and they're arguably the greatest takeaway from the movie as a whole. But this is also an entertaining action flick—a true, cinematic epic that's massive in runtime and impressive in production. It's not just the actors who were firing away on all cinematic cylinders.

Just look at the technicians, wiping their brows from behind the scenes: Gabriel Yared as the composer, John Seale as the cinematographer, and Walter Murch as the editor. They all deserve their flowers, as Yared's dulcet music punctuates some well-written dialogue, and Seale's careful camerawork catches some high-octane set pieces.

In the editing room, Walter Murch has put the finishing touches on some all-time great entries of the war genre. He may be the best of his craft thanks to *Apocalypse Now* (1979), *The English Patient* (1996), and *Jarhead* (2005). Regarding *Cold Mountain*: He pieced the project together with passion and precision, helping to create a product that was intricate in set design and steady in its filming. After Murch's work was finished, replete with surprising jump cuts and dramatic fades to black, *Cold Mountain* had its premiere and was subsequently lauded by critics.

Again, it's an epic war film, huge in its premise and even grander with execution. But Minghella had to tone things down from the story's novel counterpart, which featured nine battles overall. His adaptation has just one, and while it drew criticism from a certain corner of historians, The Battle of the Crater is nonetheless an entertaining set piece with many moving parts.

This marked the penultimate movie by writer-director Anthony Minghella, whose final film was released a few years later in the form of *Breaking and Entering* (2006). Not the most prominent of titles. But no matter: In the twentieth century, the auteur put in great film work thanks to both *The English Patient* (1996) and *The Talented Mr. Ripley* (1999), with the former going down as one of the most respected movies of its decade. It's a war film of sorts, as well, with *The English Patient* granting Minghella some unprecedented experience when painting portraits of soldiers in battle.

He even won Best Director at the Academy Awards for his efforts therein, and what's more is that he wrote the script, as well. That's typically the case with Minghella films, though. The only project under his belt for which he does not hold a screenwriting credit is *Heaven* (2002), which was released one year prior to his highly anticipated war film that features Cillian Murphy.

In the eyes of many fans, Minghella's second war film—the same number for Cillian, oddly enough—*Cold Mountain* without a doubt lived up to its mighty expectations, and that can largely be attributed to the efforts of its cast. And even if critics thought that *Cold Mountain* paled for the most part in comparison to Minghella's prior foray into the genre, they were largely positive when analyzing their consensus. With good reason.

Even historians had good things to say, citing an authenticity to the props, like the weapons of the Confederacy, as well as the overall appearance of the characters thanks to the work of famous costume designer Ann Roth. Nominated on five occasions at the Academy Awards for best Costume Design, she even won a few years prior thanks to another collaboration with Minghella—on *The English Patient*.

That's the most revered film of their respective careers, though they teamed up multiple other times such as with *The Talented Mr. Ripley*. Another nomination for Roth at the Oscars. After her work on *Cold Mountain*, for which she was arguably snubbed a nomination, Roth walked away victorious once again for her efforts on *Ma Rainey's Black Bottom* (2020). Two Academy Awards for the costume designer of *Cold Mountain* perfectly showcases the thought put into its careful portrayal of war.

This didn't just resonate with historians and pundits, though. Also film fans. It made great money at the box office, raking in more than $170 million against a $79 budget, and as a whole, even more impressive was the praise *Cold Mountain* received from critics. Famous film critic Roger Ebert awarded the film three stars out of a possible four, with Leonard Maltin going one step forward and giving *Cold Mountain* an extra half star.

Those are two of the most famous pundits in the medium's history—the cream of the criticism crop—and they both called this war film great. All that said, perhaps the biggest story re: the success of *Cold Mountain* would be its numerous nominations at the Academy Awards. Receiving recognition in six categories at the association's 76th ceremony, most of the nominations went to the aforementioned technicians: Yared, Seale, and Murch.

But there's also Jude Law, who was recognized for Best Actor. Sure, he came up short to Sean Penn in *Mystic River* (2003), but still, that showcases the prowess of the cast and crew of *Cold Mountain* that was collected for various means of production, including each of the high-profile names that portray these highly empathetic characters.

While Law was left out of a victory, there was an Oscar winner among the cast of *Cold Mountain*, and her name is Renée Zellweger. She walked away with a golden statuette in the category of Best Supporting Actress, beating names such as Holly Hunter. And with good reason. She shines as Ruby Thewes, a farmer who cares for Nicole Kidman's character Ada after her husband goes off to war.

Among the most famous thespians in Australia's rich history, Nicole Kidman appeared in five episodes of a miniseries titled *Vietnam* (1987), while later co-starring in *The Railway Man* (2013). In between those released was *Hemingway & Gellhorn* (2012), in which she played a world-famous war correspondent, but even against all those titles, perhaps her greatest contribution is *Cold Mountain*. She frankly steals several scenes as Ada, an endearingly troubled co-protagonist.

On top of her husband being absent, Ada fights against numerous other internal combatants as she recently suffered a death in the family, in the unfortunate form of her father. Not the best of times for Ada, nor for her husband: Law's character, Inman, who drives the plot on his journey to find his wife, and along the way, he's introduced to some memorable personalities.

After escaping his regime, Inman posts up for a night at the home of a woman named Sara. She's played by Natalie Portman, who should commonly be remembered as a war hero herself. Just like *Cold Mountain*, the other two examples amid Natalie Portman's filmography also classify as romance: *Brothers* (2009), and *A Tale of Love and Darkness* (2015).

In spite of some impressive appearances, however, she never gets the credit she deserves for acting against backdrops of battle. She's perhaps at her peak in *Cold Mountain* as Sara, who helps Inman elude capture in an unforgettable scene. When they wake up the following morning, Inman and Sara are greeted by three soldiers of the Union Army who are scouring the area to demand food from citizens. This is where Cillian comes into play.

It was common practice for soldiers to raid random homesteads throughout the American Civil War, as troops across the nation were starving. Rations were divided by way of some rather involved logistics, typically led by an appointed Commissary General of Subsistence. Three men held this title for the Union, each succeeding their predecessor due to the latter's respective death. For the Confederacy, the bulk of the food was allocated by Col. Lucius B. Northup, who was tasked with heavier burdens than his rivals from the Union.

The northern troops were rationed beans, peas, rice, potatoes, and cornmeal, not to mention sugar and coffee. Predominantly, they frequently feasted on an array of meats, ranging from twelve ounces of pork to four ounces of beef, depending on the day. Meanwhile, soldiers in the South were rationed primarily with food that was found from the land, such as green apples and field corn. Peanuts were abundant—their primary source of protein—and they harbored a fair amount of sugar.

The Confederacy was struggling, in other words. Starving, going mad, and scouring the lands for anything they could acquire, which often led to some dire circumstances and thereby hasty decisions. Soldiers would often raid sources of Union food—in September of 1864, the infamous Beefsteak Raid was led by the Confederate cavalry. But they'd also raid homesteads, such as with Cillian and his crew stealing chickens in *Cold Mountain*.

Typically, the soldiers that Cillian plays are honorable, stoic men with good intentions in mind for their fellow on-screen characters. That isn't the case in *Cold Mountain*—at least, not at first. Searching Sara's home for rations with Law's protagonist hiding out in the woods adjacent, Cillian's character Bardolph watches his cohorts commit atrocious acts on the single mother who's played by Portman. They hold her baby hostage, and then proceed to rape her. Not Bardolph, though.

```
Pistol heads towards the cabin. As he
approaches the door, Bardolph rearranges
the blankets to cover the baby. Pistol
opens the door. Nym is on top of Sara.
Pistol laughs, enters, and is clubbed down
by Inman, who steps out onto the porch,
while SARA SHRUGS OFF THE BODY OF NYM, HIS
THROAT CUT.
Bardolph looks up to see Inman walking
towards him. Bardolph has left his weapon
by the fence.
```

```
                    INMAN

        Move away from the baby.

Bardolph obeys, terrified. Sara runs out,
collects Ethan,gives  a  little  moan  of
anguish, runs back inside the cabin.
```

He takes an anxious seat and stares in terror at the crimes against humanity that are unfolding before his eyes. Confusion, fear, sadness—multiple emotions overcome Bardolph's countenance, and it's apparent that he means no real harm to Sara, nor to her newborn baby. He's just hungry. They haven't eaten in days.

Unfortunately for Bardolph and fans of Cillian Murphy, the mother doesn't care. After the protagonist forces the rapists off of Sara and shoots them where they stand, he opts to let Bardolph run free. As for Sara, on the other hand, well—she picks up a rifle and shoots him down without a thought or hesitation.

Just one scene for Cillian here in *Cold Mountain*, but an admirable showing, nonetheless. And in his second film of the genre, his death was once again noteworthy. These aren't your typical war casualties: Every scene in which Cillian is killed is presented as a spectacle, and each of the sequences play prominent parts in the plot.

```
                  BARDOLPH

Don't shoot me, please. We're starving.
We haven't eaten.


                    INMAN

You'd better get running before you
catch your death of cold.
```

```
                    BARDOLPH
     (nods, terrified)
     Thanks, thank you. I will.
     AND THEN A SHOT RINGS OUT AND HE CRASHES
     TO THE GROUND, DEAD.
     Behind Inman, Sara stands with a rifle.
```

As for *Cold Mountain*: Though not for Cillian's character—nor for Inman, the protagonist—the story does conclude on something of a high note. Inman dies in the arms of the woman he loves, and it's revealed that he's the father of Ada's newborn girl, whose name is revealed to be Grace. After a lengthy runtime of brutalities and struggle, the film fades to black with the family eating lunch.

Though not the most conventional of war films you'll read about today—more focused on romance than hard-hitting action—and by no means an important performance from Cillian's overall career, it is relevant in hindsight given his status as the greatest soldier in cinema. Sure, he appears for a single scene in *Cold Mountain*. But like his character Bardolph attempted with Sara's food, the scene is certainly stolen by Cillian. Either way—regardless of the role's prominence—*Cold Mountain* does nothing but bolster his resume as the greatest war actor ever.

Among the most famous films by Anthony Minghella, the auteur dedicated five years of his life to the creation of *Cold Mountain*—after the scriptwriting process, the movie was shot in Romania, where the weather conditions brought about certain travails to production. Once filming was complete, Minghella toiled away in the editing room for an entire year. For that process of post-production alone, he and Walter Murch deserve much more credit from fans.

But their efforts paid off in many respects, evident by its numbers of success. It's a high-profile film that only pushed Cillian further toward the center on the map of Hollywood prominence. Blockbusters will prove beneficial to most any actor's career, and luckily for Cillian following the release of *Cold Mountain*, he teamed up with Christopher Nolan, who would go on to make waves at the box office like few directors to ever live.

The first credit of Cillian's to come after his blockbuster war drama was the even more famous *Batman Begins* (2005), directed by Christopher Nolan. One of the most renowned comic book movies ever made, its script was co-written by the aforementioned auteur with the help of David S. Goyer. Those are a pair of well-known names, particularly Nolan, and the same can be said for the film's lead star: Christian Bale, who donned the mask and cape to portray the eponymous DC superhero.

To this point, *Batman Begins* was the most lucrative project that Cillian had ever appeared in, and frankly, those numbers are hardly close. Previously, the highest-grossing movie to feature Cillian Murphy was actually his second stint on the battlefield, *Cold Mountain* by Anthony Minghella. Even then, though—*Batman Begins* was twice as successful, accruing $373.7 million against a $150 million budget.

On top of garnering more recognition for the budding Irish superstar thanks to its success in theaters, the superhero origin story *Batman Begins* also features Cillian in a much more prominent role than his prior blockbuster *Cold Mountain*. Throughout the years, nobody has shone light on the caliber of Cillian nearly to the extent of Chris, and that shows in their first encounter more than most films thereafter.

Marking their first collaboration with one another, *Batman Begins* also introduced the director to actors like Christian Bale, as well as Michael Caine. In the sequels to this reboot of the famous DC comic book adaptations, both Bale and Caine reprise their roles as Bruce Wayne and his loyal butler Alfred, and as fate would have it, both of those world-renowned performers have served meaningful time on the battlefields of cinema.

Both of them debuted with war films, in fact: *A Hill in Korea* (1956) for Caine, and *Empire of the Sun* (1987) for Bale. The former would go on to appear in such examples as *Foxhole in Cairo* (1960), *Zulu* (1964), *Play Dirty* (1969), *Battle of Britain* (1969), *Too Late the Hero* (1970), *The Eagle Has Landed* (1976).

Perhaps his greatest claim to war movie fame would be *A Bridge Too Far* (1977), but of course, all of those titles were released well before Nolan ever came into the picture of Caine's career. Even after their collaborations, the actor would portray a WWII veteran named Bernard Jordan in his final film role ever. Called *The Great Escaper* (2023), it put a tremendous capstone on an impressive career, with Caine actually being a veteran himself of the Korean War.

As for Bale: Just one year after *Batman Begins*, he played a Vietnam veteran in *Rescue Dawn* (2006), and in the following decade, he doubled his output with *The Flowers of War* (2011) and *The Promise* (2016). None of those are commonly considered as classics, or anything. Not like *Batman Begins* with the talented Michael Caine.

They both perform brilliantly throughout the trilogy, but also appearing throughout each entry therein is the talented actor at hand. Arguably the three greatest actors among Nolan's recurring stable, Cillian, Christian, and Michael; each performed brilliantly in their respectively well-known roles. The Irishman plays Jonathan Crane—more famously remembered as Scarecrow—a role he'd go on to play two more times while under Nolan's direction, albeit to lesser extents.

Though Scarecrow didn't play prominent parts in either *The Dark Knight* (2008) or *The Dark Knight Rises* (2012), he provided such indelible efforts in the trilogy's first entry that Nolan essentially had no choice: He had to include Cillian among their respective casts. Two of the most famous film collaborators of the twenty-first century, Cillian and Christopher, have provided film fans with some of the most memorable silver-screen moments in modern movie history, and *Batman Begins* kicked things into motion.

For what it's worth, Liam Neeson plays Ra's al Ghul, with that fellow Irishman boasting a few war movies worth writing home about. In back-to-back years, he appeared in a pair of WWII movies: *Shining Through* (1992) and *Schindler's List* (1993). He then played the eponymous protagonist in *Michael Collins* (1996), solidifying himself as a bona fide genre hero. He isn't exactly a staple of Nolan's stable, though. Without a doubt, Cillian, Christian, and Michael were the ones that clicked with the director, and in that regard, there are also a couple of technicians worth noting. Take Hans Zimmer, for instance.

He's worked on six occasions with Chris, and like the aforementioned actors, *Batman Begins* was their first collaboration. Same thing goes for Lee Smith, as well—after their comic book adaptation, Smith would edit the next six movies that Christopher directed, with *Batman Begins* remaining one of his all-time best. Across the board, everyone involved was thankfully sent their flowers.

On top of its resonance with critics and its widespread success in theaters, *Batman Begins* remains a salient entry in Christopher's filmography for acquainting him with each of his greatest collaborators. From Cillian Murphy and Michael Caine to Christian Bale and Hans Zimmer, everyone involved in *Batman Begins* was essential to its production.

A behind-the-scenes creative that Nolan had worked with previously was the cinematographer, whose name is Wally Pfister. This was his third-straight movie that he shot for Christopher Nolan, and the latter's fourth feature film in general. After shooting his debut *Following* by his lonesome, Nolan recruited Pfister, who sat behind their camera for *Memento* (2000) and continued for well over a decade.

And with regard to *Batman Begins*, it's worth noting that Wally was the only name among the cast and crew who received an Oscar nomination. At the 78th Academy Awards, he was in the running for Best Cinematography. And although he came up short, Wally

Pfister would walk away victorious just five years thereafter for yet another Christopher Nolan film.

At this point, no matter the craft—whether the respective teammate is an actor or more of a technician—Cillian is among the director's most famous and frequent collaborators. Similar to his experience under Danny Boyle's direction, he says he had seen Nolan's films before working with him, calling himself a "huge fan" of both *Following* and *Memento*.

He was eager to work with the director, and in the inaugural entry of the superhero trilogy, Cillian auditioned for Batman. After that fell through, he and Nolan discussed some other roles, and the two decided on Scarecrow. It was then that Cillian read a few of the early *Batman* comics in preparation for his portrayal, and clearly, his research paid off in spades.

From Riddler and Poison Ivy to Penguin and Mr. Freeze, the *Batman* movies of Hollywood past by Tim Burton and Joel Schumacher featured a wide array of villains from the celebrated comic series. Even the majority of enemies from Nolan's trilogy had been previously depicted by those well-known directors, like Catwoman in *Batman Returns* (1992), Two-Face in *Batman Forever* (1995), and Bane in *Batman and Robin* (1997).

Throughout all those characters, their respective actors and films, the nightmarish Scarecrow has only been played in live-action films by one performer in history: Cillian Murphy, and he shows up in all three Nolan movies with an unambiguous understanding of the lionized source material. It wouldn't be for a few more years before he reprised the role, but in the meantime, in the same year as *Batman Begins*, he branched out to a couple of archetypes atypical of his career.

Directed by Wes Craven from Carl Ellsworth's script, *Red Eye* (2005) features Cillian in the co-starring role. While traveling to Miami on a red-eye flight, hotel manager Lisa Reisert—the protagonist, portrayed by Rachel McAdams—finds herself caught up in a plot to assassinate the Deputy Secretary of Homeland Security.

His name is Charles Keefe – he's staying with his family at the Lux Atlantic Hotel, the facility that's managed by Lisa. She's heading back to Miami where the hotel is located, but before boarding her flight, she acquaints herself with Cillian, who shows up as Jackson Rippner. As the terrorist in charge of the assassination, Rippner uses his silver tongue to flirt with the protagonist, but once they're aboard the red eye, he reveals his true intentions.

It's a thrilling plot, primarily thanks to Ellsworth's script. Although he put great work into television before the release of *Red Eye*, this marked his feature-length debut in terms of screenwriting. He's not a director like Wes, though. Known primarily for his horror movies like *A Nightmare on Elm Street* (1984) and *Scream* (1996), that world-famous filmmaker is a master of suspense, boasting great understanding of direction in tandem with a keen ear for dialogue.

From the very first frame of *Red Eye*, Craven directed his cast with passion as they deliver endlessly memorable dialogue that's embedded with humor, poignancy, and subtext. That's primarily thanks to Ellsworth, but another name among the crew who rendered *Red Eye* a success was Marco Beltrami, the composer.

A close collaborator of director Wes Craven, he'd scored such films as the first two *Scream* entries, as well as *Cursed* (2005) in the same year as *Red Eye*. Without a doubt, the psychological thriller set primarily on a plane was their greatest project of the year, and perhaps since the second *Scream* film.

While *Cursed* failed both critically and commercially, *Red Eye* soared through the clearest skies of reception when it was initially released by DreamWorks back in 2005. This proved to be the busiest year of Cillian's career, nominated at the Irish Film & Television Awards for both his appearance in *Batman Begins*, and his co-starring work in *Red Eye*. He came up short for both, but still. Two nominations in a single year is a rare and impressive feat.

Even still, Cillian had one more appearance left in his measureless tank of performing. Enter: Neil Jordan, one of the greatest filmmakers to ever be born in Ireland. He made a name for himself with his third feature film, titled *Mona Lisa* (1986), and in the following decade, Jordan won Best Original Screenplay at the Academy Awards for his indelible efforts on *The Crying Game* (1992).

Throughout his critically acclaimed career, Jordan has directed some of the most prolific actors in the history of Ireland, such as Brendan Gleeson, Liam Neeson, Colin Farrell, and Stephen Rea. Then, there's Cillian Murphy. For his performance as Patrick "Kitten" Braden, a transgender Irish woman in *Breakfast on Pluto* (2005), he received his first nomination at the Golden Globes, one for Best Actor – Motion Picture Musical or Comedy. Quite the mouthful, and although he came up short to Joaquin Phoenix in *Walk the Line* (2006), that nomination renders *Breakfast on Pluto* a pivotal project from the career of Cillian Murphy.

He said he was in love with the book on which the film is based, and once he heard Neil Jordan was adapting it, he annoyed the director until he was granted an audition. He calls the filming of *Breakfast on Pluto* a "formative experience," and he refers to Kitten a character that he "has a deep, deep affection for."

In spite of some positive qualities around every corner of production, he undoubtedly stole the show of *Breakfast on Pluto*. At the Irish Film and Television Awards—after being nominated at the ceremony four times in the previous four years—the performer of the hour was victorious in the category of Best Actor. About time. Meanwhile, also at the IFTA, filmmaker Neil Jordan walked away with a win for Best Director, and what's more is that Jordan also won Best Script, an award that he shared with co-writer Patrick McCabe.

Although *Breakfast on Pluto* isn't the greatest film from any of those names, it is among the best of Cillian's silver-screen efforts, and it allowed him to work with some of his country's greatest talents. In the following year, he appeared in a short film that boasted a crew also comprised of Irish filmmaking royalty. What's more, *The Silent City* (2006) by Ruairi Robinson features Cillian as a soldier.

The Old City Limits:
Playing a Soldier in a Short Film

After taking a brief break from the battlefield, Cillian returned guns blazing with two roles in a single year. Granted, one of those performances as a soldier was within a short film. But *The Silent City* is nonetheless a high-quality piece of storytelling, and Cillian's character is credited simply as "Soldier" —couldn't be more relevant.

Written and directed by Ruairi Robinson, the short runs for just under six minutes, not including the credits. On top of writing and directing the product, Ruairí Robinson also edited *The Silent City*, and handled the visual effects. This is typically the case for Ruairí, who even voiced the eponymous character in his hit short *BlinkyTM* (2011).

As a filmmaker, Ruairí is primarily known for this format, silver-screen stories that fall on the shorter end of the spectrum. At the 74th Academy Awards, he even received a nomination for Best Animated Short Film for *Fifty Percent Grey* (2001). Though he didn't receive the same praise for *The Silent City* with Cillian Murphy, this science fiction short is still on the same level.

Little dialogue can be heard in the opening sequences—quickly rendering "The Silent City" an apropos title for the project—as a trio of soldiers traverse the desolation of a battlefield that acts as both an atmospheric setting, and as a medium for exposition. Evident by the death and destruction that encircles every step of its three featured characters, *The Silent City* is divided into the post-apocalyptic subgenre.

Co-stars and compatriots Don Wycherley and Garvan McGrath perform well as his fellow soldiers, while most prominently worth noting re: the names of *The Silent City* would be the talent behind the scenes. Director of photography Robbie Ryan has worked with some of the greatest filmmakers of their respective generations, from Andrea Arnold and Ken Loach to Stephen Frears and Noah Baumbach.

He's also shot two films for Yorgos Lanthimos, starting with *The Favorite* (2018). For his unrivaled shot value and careful movements, Robbie Ryan was nominated for Best Cinematography at the 91st Academy Awards. A few years later, he'd replicate that success with *Poor Things* (2023), also by Yorgos Lanthimos.

Though not nearly as popular as those feature-length masterworks, he does pull out all of the stops in *The Silent City* that put him on the map in the first place. Before ever shooting a big-budget feature, Robbie Ryan held credits on critically-acclaimed shorts such as *Wasp* (2003) and *Antonio's Breakfast* (2005), and has even held the camera for multiple shorts that were made by Nick Ryan, his cousin.

Another member of short film royalty, Nick even holds a production credit on *The Silent City*. A lot of names worth noting, and even then, the Ryan cousins are only scratching the surface of this committed and talented crew. Modeling of the cityscapes were handled by Ed Bruce, while John O'Connell was in charge of soldier modeling and particle effects. Excellent work on all accounts.

Then, there's Michael McCarthy, who led the process of rotoscoping—a technique that's typically used with animated projects. It involves an artist tracing over live-action footage to create movements that are truer to life than traditional animation, and in the case of *The Silent City*, rotoscoping is used in conjunction with the visual effects to digitally compose the actors into the apocalyptic setting.

It's an involved process that paid off in spades with regard to the short film at hand, and since the release of *The Silent City*, rotoscoping has evolved to blend live-action shots with computer-generated imagery. The first title to do this was a Netflix-produced miniseries, called *The Liberator* (2020)—a war drama, oddly enough.

On the other hand, *The Silent City* isn't your conventional war film. It's more science-fiction, than anything, with characters adorning high-tech armor while traversing a landscape that's been ravaged by an unspecified event of clearly apocalyptic proportions. But the grounds they're patrolling is also a war zone, defined by the disarray of battle and interspersed with anti-personnel explosives that kick off the events of the plot.

On what appears to be a patrol route, a trip mine is triggered by the trio of soldiers—Cillian's character, to be specific, who's one of two parties that gets injured by the devastating blast. The third, unscathed soldier calls for backup, and the film's perspective shifts to an unidentified object somewhere else in the city, stalking the graveyard of what seems to be his former prey: Captain Smith, whom the soldier is calling for backup.

The film ends with the soldier's voice dubbed over a frantic point-of-view shot, adding a tangible sense of ambiguity to a piece of storytelling that's primarily focused on the development of atmosphere. But world-class technique went into *The Silent City* well before the change in perspective, with behind-the-scenes names like Robbie Ryan and Michael McCarthy producing some truly powerful results.

Across the board of production, really, *The Silent City* hits home: Abrupt cuts in continuity are well balanced with dramatic fades to black, and engaging shot value is facilitated by the characters who use a handheld mirror to check their corners when navigating the battlefield. There's also a vigorous, original score—thanks in large part to cellist Rory Pierce—and formidable tactics of sound design by virtue of Gavin Little.

With a thought-provoking story and jaw-dropping visuals, *The Silent City* was quite a hit as far as short films are concerned. It even boasts an accolade from an Irish award association, one that's dedicated entirely to short films: The Golden Blasters. They're the National Irish Science Fiction Awards that are presented annually at Octocon.

Within a Valley Green: Starring in a Revered War Movie

itten by Paul Laverty with Ken Loach as the director, *The Wind*
at Shakes the Barley won the Palme d'Or at the 2006 Cannes Film
tival, and it's easy to see why. Offering tremendous insight into
human condition's complexity, *The Wind That Shakes the Barley*
ins in the middle of an intense match of hurling, with indistinct
uts from the characters being drowned out by George Fenton's
e, and the hasty movements of the game being captured by the
ful camerawork of Barry Ackroyd.

oon after he finishes his hurling match, Cillian's lead charac-
vitnesses a summary execution as his friend Micheál is killed
group of British soldiers. With an on-screen presence like few
s of his generation—especially in war films, which feature set-
and scenarios that always seems to highlight his caliber—Cil-
eacts with heartfelt emotion and puts forth a perfect portrayal
protagonist, a medical student named Damien O'Donovan.

s his initial goal, Damien is preparing to undergo his training
don, leaving soon after the plot kicks off. From the second he
his mouth and says his goodbyes around the village, Cillian
ms with poise and passion, putting pure poignance on dis-
efore he ever steps foot on the battlefield. The plot truly kicks
er Damien witnesses the execution of his friend, and decides
ar himself into the ranks of the Irish Republican Army.

low Irish actor Pádraic Delaney, who's rather unknown today,
s as Damien's brother, Teddy O'Donovan. He's in charge of
gade of which Damien now fights for, with the group set-
to retrieve enough revolvers to assassinate a few auxiliaries
oyal Irish Constabulary. In a casual sense, these volunteers
own as auxies, while the constables were called Black and

In turn, Octocon is a national science fiction conve
hosted annually in Dublin. On top of sci-fi, the awards i
ror shorts, and fantasy films. Obviously, *The Silent City*
of those categories, and in many respects, there are hori
as well. Either way, *The Silent City* was eligible, and ii
inaugural ceremony, Ruairi Robinson won the (somev
Golden Blaster. Well-earned, as the writer-director c
inventive short that resonated fondly with fans.

The primary actors deserve flowers, as well—for
as the project may be, they carried out their tasks as i
ing the trenches of battle. They're dedicated to the h
characters bestow, performing perfectly as a trio c
each harbor distinct personalities.

Without a doubt, the soldier is Cillian's all-time
type, indicated not just by the aforementioned sho
Robinson, but also *The Wind That Shakes the Barl*
ture film in which Cillian plays the lead. It was his
a movie within the genre at hand, and for many
most critically acclaimed war film that Cillian Mu
Regardless of genre—and on top of featuring an
acting from the Irishman at hand—it's also one of
acclaimed movies of the entire twenty-first centu

W
Th
Fe
the
beg
sho
sco
car

ter
by a
acto
ting:
lian
as th
A
in Lo
open
perfo
play l
off aff
to swe
Fe
co-sta
the br
ting of
of the
were k

Tans after the colors of their uniforms—though, for what it's worth, the "black" was more of a green that appeared to be darker than it was in reality.

As a group of British conscripts, the primary goal of the Black and Tans was to halt any sense of progression for the Irish Republican Army. These recruits weren't trained in proper policing methods, however, which lead to unprovoked attacks on civilians and their possessions. Nonetheless, their methods were often effective, as was the case in *The Wind That Shakes the Barley*. As the plan of the primary character unfolds, the brigade is caught and arrested. Inside his jail cell is when Damien meets Dan, a train driver played by the talented Liam Cunningham.

For those unfamiliar: Cunningham made a name for himself in movies like *A Little Princess* (1995), *Jude* (1996), and *Dog Soldiers* (2002). Most commonly, though, Cunningham is known for his efforts as Ser Davos Seaworth in the hit fantasy series *Game of Thrones* (2011–2019). He gives one of his all-time greatest performances here in *The Wind That Shakes the Barley*, even winning Best Supporting Actor at the Irish Film and Television Awards.

After production, Cunningham commented on how much the movie taught him about the history of his own nation. Referring to both Ken Loach and the film in general, he stated, "It took an Englishman to come over for me to force me in the position to examine my own history." Raw emotion is only part of what's on display by the entire cast and crew—*The Wind That Shakes the Barley* is also an honest and accurate depiction of the brutal afflictions of war.

Great attention to detail went into every corner of production. For example: All of the British soldiers were played by real-life members of an Irish Army Reserve unit. The ex-British army soldiers who acted under Ken Loach's competent direction were instructed to downplay their theatricals, ignoring the cameras and acting just as they would when executing searches, interrogations, and the like.

Although Murphy is perhaps the film's biggest takeaway—more on his performance in a bit—Ken Loach deserves all the flowers in the world for the essential work he put forth, even hiring a historical consultant to advise him on the tales of yore. The historian's name was Dr. Donal Ó Drisceoil, who worked at University College Cork, and together, the two painted a precise portrait of the Irish Civil War.

The film's title is also historically relevant, taken from Robert Dwyer Joyce's song of the same name. Heard early on in the film, the tune features a line that reads, "the wind that shakes the barley." After the song was first released, that titular lyric became a motif throughout the culture and antiquity of Ireland. It even had a film named after it.

```
I sat within the valley green
I sat me with my true love
My sad heart strove the two between
The old love and the new love
The old for her, the new that made
Me think on Ireland dearly
While soft the wind blew down the glade
And shook the golden barley
```

Set during the Irish Rebellion of 1798, the song plays out from the first-person outlook of a love-stricken insurgent from Wexford—one of only two counties (the other being Carlow) that saw any sort of success from a military perspective during the aforementioned conflict. The United Irishmen were greatly outnumbered by the forces of Great Britain, nearly two to one.

When on marches, the Irish rebels would store grains in their pockets as provisions: not just oat, but barley, as well. By the time the war was done, more than half of the rebels had perished – about 30,000, as surmised by historians—most of whom were buried on the outskirts of the battlefield. Bodies of fallen rebels would be thrown into unmarked graves, and after the shifting of seasons, patches of barley began springing in the soil. From harvested grains left as provisions in rebel pockets to the cultivation of golden plants that shook softly in the wind.

This classic, modern war film from the uncompromising Ken Loach will leave an indelible impact via harrowing scenes of torture and high-octane gunfights. A bloody affair to be sure, but entirely worth the heartache those deaths will elicit thanks to the script's meaningful development of character, as well as the themes that are produced so seamlessly therefrom. Written by Ken Loach's long-time collaborator Paul Laverty, it features dynamic dialogue that's delivered at a rapid yet soothing pace by every member of the cast, particularly Cillian Murphy.

While dealing with the travails of battle, his protagonist Damien is balancing a relationship with Sinéad, who's played by Orla Fitzgerald. Though not the most notable name among Ireland's rich history of film, she's worth noting regarding Cillian's career, as they had previously acted alongside one another in *Disco Pigs*, the play by Enda Walsh. Already having established a tangible rapport as performers, their romantically involved characters highlight the war film at hand as they exchange well-written dialogue.

On top of their dulcet nature, there's also legitimate subtext featured in each of the emotional exchanges, and on occasion, the poignancy is punctuated by an amiable style of humor. Maybe a bit of romance. Oftentimes, some thrills. Around every corner of its plot, *The Wind That Shakes the Barley* runs a wonderful gamut of emotion, and the plot is perfectly paced until the fireworks of its finale.

Though it's hard to stomach, Damien's death is worth delving into, as well. Gunned down by numerous soldiers at once, much like the leaders of the Easter Rising whom Cillian referred to in his author note. His character suffers a horrible demise, but in honorable fashion – just as Cillian was committed to his performance,

Damien was devout in his actions, truly dedicated to a consequential cause in which he instilled his wholehearted faith.

In terms of his war films and perhaps his career in general, this is the most gut-wrenching scene in which Cillian's character was killed, executed in broad daylight by the ruthless gunplay of a firing squad. It's a brutal death for anyone, but what's worse, the shots were authorized by Damien's brother, Teddy. Heartbreaking stuff, with *The Wind That Shakes the Barley* painting an intensely emotional portrait of war until its final gut-wrenching frame: Damien's lifeless body hanging limply from a post to which his withered wrists are tied.

```
But blood for blood without remorse,
I've ta'en at Oulart Hollow
And placed my true love's clay-cold
corpse
Where I full soon will follow;
And 'round her grave I wander drear,
Noon, night, and morning early,
With breaking heart whene'er I hear
The wind that shakes the barley!
```

Among the finest war films of the twenty-first century, Ken Loach's critical darling may stand tall as Cillian's most notable claim to fame. At least, when it comes to his war films. He's the best actor the genre's ever seen, the greatest soldier in cinema, and due to both the quality of his performance as well as the film itself, that's in large part thanks to *The Wind That Shakes the Barley*.

In his *GQ* interview, Cillian said he's quite proud of the work he put into it *The Wind That Shakes the Barley*, even homing in on his admiration for the director. "As an Irishman, and as an actor," he said, "it was a great privilege to work with Ken Loach." In his cast note, Cillian expanded on his understanding of the iconic character he portrayed, and he continued singing the praises of the brilliance of Ken Loach.

This was the director's sixth time working with screenwriter Paul Laverty, with the two crafting an endlessly touching tale about a pivotal point in Irish history. Another collaborator of Loach is cameraman Barry Ackroyd, with *The Wind That Shakes the Barley* being their eleventh film with one another. The cinematographer even went on to shoot *The Hurt Locker* by Kathryn Bigelow—another essential war film of the twenty-first century that boasts notable shot value from a veteran of the genre.

There's one more collaborator of Ken's who's worth noting, and his name is George Fenton. A famous English composer, he had previously scored nine of Loach's most essential titles, and aside from their work with one another, Fenton has put forth tremendous efforts alongside other high-profile filmmakers such as Richard Attenborough, Nora Ephron, Terry Gilliam, and Neil Jordan.

He's even been nominated for five Academy Awards—in any other year, Fenton could've been recognized for *The Wind That Shakes the Barley*, as well. His efforts worked in wonderful tandem with every other facet of high-quality filmmaking at play, from the camerawork of Ackroyd to the editing of Jonathan Morris.

Though not the most famous war film you'll read about today, it did accrue admirable numbers with regard to overall ticket sales. At the worldwide box office, *The Wind That Shakes the Barley* raked in $25.7 million against an $8 million budget. It tripled its worth, and for a time, those results rendered *TWTSTB* the most lucrative independent film to ever be produced in Ireland.

It's since been overtaken by *The Guard* (2009), written and directed by John Michael McDonough, but still—name value aside—*The Wind That Shakes the Barley* was highly revered by historians, pundits, and hardcore fans alike. Across the board of reception, audiences hold this Ken Loach war film in the utmost of regards, and justifiably so.

Filling in for Roger Ebert, editor Jim Emerson awarded four stars out of four, and cited it "among the best war films ever made." Pretty high praise, and he wasn't wrong. What's more is that *The Wind That Shakes the Barley* won the Palme d'Or at the 59th Cannes Film Festival, one of cinema's most prestigious achievements. It came out victorious over world-famous movies like *Babel* (2006), *Marie Antoinette* (2006), *Pan's Labyrinth* (2006), and *Volver* (2006)—pretty impressive, and to be frank, that's only scratching the surface of the accolades accrued by *The Wind That Shakes the Barley*.

At the 60th British Academy Film Awards, the actor at hand was nominated in the Rising Star category. Sure, he came up short to Eva Green for her work in *Casino Royale*, but still. A simple nomination at the BAFTAs is worth writing home about, and even then, that's just the most prominent association in which Cillian Murphy was recognized.

The European Film Awards, the British Independent Spirit Awards, the Irish Film & Television Awards—no matter the ceremony, and regardless if he won or lost, each nomination was well-earned by Cillian. Even playing a fictional character, his performances in the genre give audiences a glimpse into the brutal characteristics of war, and his charisma shines light into the darkness thereof.

To this day, *The Wind That Shakes the Barley* is among the best (and most important) titles from his long and famous career. Upon release, the movie was especially in vogue. It didn't quite garner him the status of a household name, but over the coming years, he took a break from the war genre and received widespread recognition in the process.

Nearly one decade into his career, Cillian began consistently appearing in the biggest and best films of the century. Some of the titles from this period are highly underrated, and even if the given title holds significant name value, it's likely that the individual effort from Cillian is undervalued in itself. In some instances, he deserves more credit for both—the quality of the respective film, and the power of his performance.

Just one year after he appeared in Loach's acclaimed war stint, Cillian landed another leading part in *Sunshine* (2007), along with *Watching the Detectives* (2007). Although it features Cillian Murphy in a co-starring role alongside popular actress Lucy Liu, the latter isn't really worth noting. On the opposite end of the spectrum of relevance, *Sunshine* is a top-tier sci-fi thriller, and once again, it features Murphy in the primary role. By far, it's the most prominent movie of his from that year, and although its numbers of success may imply otherwise, it remains one of the finest titles of his entire career.

On paper, just in terms of its premise, the plot to *Sunshine* is fairly straightforward. The year is 2057, and a physicist named Robert Kapa—the protagonist, who's played by Cillian—is tasked with leading an expedition that's essential to the future of life on Earth. The Sun is dying, and thus, mankind is presented with the premise of total annihilation.

Embarking on a life-or-death quest to reignite the star, Robert gathers a group of seven specialists and sets off to outer space. Directed by Danny Boyle from Alex Garland's script, *Sunshine* marked Cillian's second time collaborating with that writer-director duo following their work on *28 Days Later*, when they survived the apocalyptic landscape of the unhesitating undead. Now, teammates Cillian, Danny, and Alex are traversing the expansive depths of a dangerous outer space.

He shares a comedic chemistry with Chris Evans, a remarkable rapport with Rose Byrne, and a dogged dynamic with everyone else. A few of Cillian's other co-stars include Michelle Yeong, Cliff Curtis, and Benedict Wong, along with Mark Strong and his old friend Paloma Baeza. Around every corner of this star-studded cast, each performer shows up with one mission in mind: Sell the absurdity of *Sunshine* to film fans.

As they struggle to save mankind, Kapa and his crew discover some distressing skeletons in the closet of their mission. What unfolds is a thrilling adventure through the vast void of space, with *Sunshine* going down as one of the finest films from everyone involved. Given its status as a box office bomb, it's due for a cult following at any point in time.

Like his previous collaboration with Boyle, this Cillian Murphy classic is hard to get a hold of with regard to physical copies. Sure, it's attainable on streaming services—unlike *28 Days*, you can rent it online for $3.99—and if UMD versions are perhaps your preference, you could pick up a copy for Sony's PlayStation Portable. But aside from that, if you happen to own *Sunshine* on DVD or Blu-ray, grab ahold of your copies and hold on for dear life, as if dangling from a spaceship with a puncture in your suit.

On top of marking his reunion with Alex the writer and Danny the director, the sci-fi thriller *Sunshine* is further worth noting regarding Cillian's career due to it being the initial instance of him showing up as a physicist. Just like his award-winning portrayal of J. Robert Oppenheimer with his all-time greatest collaborator, Cillian showcased great commitment to his role as Robert Kapa, the "silent outsider" of a primary character.

That's how the actor viewed the protagonist, having spoken numerous times throughout the years regarding his work on *Sunshine*. Referring to the film's entire team, Cillian said they tried to "make a film that was a sci-fi blockbuster that was actually looking at themes a little bit more sophisticated." Considering the topics it tackles, they without a doubt encompassed an overarching sense of sophistication with *Sunshine* as a whole.

Though perhaps in a subtle way, this performance lent Cillian grand experience when, nearly two decades later, he won the Academy Award. Very similar characters, at least on paper—and no, not because they're both named Robert. Of course, Kapa (fictionally) and Oppenheimer (historically) are physicists. And well before he brought the latter back to life, Cillian put in tremendous research—working closely with a real-life scientist by the name of Brian Cox—

and parlayed the information into his inaugural role as a physicist named Robert.

He went on after *Sunshine* to appear once again as the infamous Jonathan Crane, and this time, it was in an all-time great of twenty-first century cinema, a world-famous movie known as *The Dark Knight* (2008). Often regarded as one of the best adaptations of a comic book to ever hit the silver screen, it launched Cillian even closer to the center of Hollywood's map where many of his *Dark Knight* co-stars had already been charted.

In his second performance under the complexity of Nolan's direction, Cillian opens the movie opposite Christian Bale's protagonist, with the former actor having worked with the director two times prior to this world-famous blockbuster. Three legendary collaborators taking part in a high-octane action scene that's well-remembered by fans of the trilogy.

Even the work from the Irishman is held in high regard, though at this point in the franchise, Scarecrow had essentially exited with regard to overall prominence. No matter how long he's in a given Batman movie, Cillian is always there, looming in the alleyways of Gotham City as an endlessly iconic supervillain.

While his role in the trilogy's prior installment facilitated far more screen time, *The Dark Knight* was actually more successful than its *Batman Begins* counterpart. Higher scores at the box office, greater acclaim by critics. Of course, the first film in Nolan's trilogy is still of the utmost quality. But *The Dark Knight* is truly a once-in-a-lifetime project, widely regarded today as one of the finest films of the century, and even of all time.

Sad to say, those superlatives don't apply to the following movie of Cillian's career: a romantic drama called *The Edge of Love* (2008). Despite being made with world-class technique of cinematography, screenwriting, direction, and editing—and although it features graceful efforts from a star-studded cast—*The Edge of Love* came up short with both film fans and critics.

With any other biography about Cillian Murphy, this movie could very well be glossed over. But with an emphasis on armed combat thanks to a soldier who's played by the Irishman, it becomes a pertinent point of discussion with regard to films about war. Considering it's also a pivotal performance from the thespian at hand, *The Edge of Love* is rendered all the more important.

The Boy is Screaming: Playing a Character With PTSD

At the onset of World War II, famous Welsh poet Dylan Thomas skirted compulsory military service by citing "an unreliable lung" and was thus assigned a Grade III classification. In other words, he was low on the list of potential draftees. Suffering from bronchitis and asthma since childhood, Thomas quickly determined that the front lines were no place for his services. But while his friends were off at war, Thomas was battling some enemies of his own, experiencing active service both personally and professionally.

Marred by adultery, alcohol abuse, artistic jealousy and more, the marriage of Welsh poet Dylan Thomas and English writer Caitlin Macnamara was much like a war zone in itself. As was Dylan's writing process. Many of the poet's pieces even revolved around the prospect of armed combat, like *I Have Longed to Move Away* and *Ceremony After a Fire Raid*. They deal heavily with themes of love, loss, and a forgotten sense of purpose, as do most of the verses under Dylan's belt of poems.

```
Do not go gentle into that good night,
Old age should burn and rave at close of day;
Rage, rage against the dying of the light.

Though wise men at their end know dark is right,
Because their words had forked no lightning they
Do not go gentle into that good night.
```

With John Maybury in the director's chair, *The Edge of Love* was written by Sharman Macdonald, who was mostly known for her stage plays before this wartime biopic. In fact, *The Edge of Love* is the only screenplay under her belt as a writer. She wrote the script from an idea by Rebekah Gilbertson, who holds a production credit, with Macdonald also basing some of the plot points on *Dylan Thomas: A Farm, Two Mansions and a Bungalow*—a book by David N. Thomas.

She recruited her daughter Keira Knightley to star as the alluring Vera Phillips, while Matthew Rhys appears as Dylan and Sienne Miller plays his wife, Caitlin. Then, there's Cillian's character: an officer in the British army by the name of William Killick. This is the first soldier played by Cillian that showed tangible effects of post-traumatic stress, which often comes into play throughout his career on the battlefield.

```
Good men, the last wave by, crying how bright
Their frail deeds might have danced in a green bay,
Rage, rage against the dying of the light.

Wild men who caught and sang the sun in flight,
And learn, too late, they grieved it on its way,
Do not go gentle into that good night.
```

Director John Maybury leads the cast with a keen understanding of the genre, drawing out one of the greatest efforts from the career of Keira Knightley, who's actually a recurring actress of war movies. Just one year prior to Maybury's entry, she co-starred in a critical darling called *Atonement* (2007)—another hybrid of romance.

She's entirely endearing in *The Edge of Love*, and the same thing goes for Sienne Miller. Another war actress, as fate would have it. This marked her first stint of service, followed by two in the following decade: *American Sniper* (2014), and *The Catcher Was a Spy* (2018). Some famous titles, leaving *The Edge of Love* as her most underrated.

It's some adept directing from Maybury, who debuted in the previous decade by way of *Love is the Devil: Study for a Portrait of Francis Bacon* (1998). It featured a breakthrough performance from

Daniel Craig, who worked with Cillian one year later on *The Trench* by Billy Boyd. After his debut, Maybury followed up with *The Jacket* (2005), starring Adrien Brody and Keira Knightley.

Having already directed Knightley once before, Maybury was familiar with her skills in front of a camera, her comprehensible prowess as a leading lady of cinema. In *The Edge of Love*, with Cillian Murphy by their side, the genius of those collaborators is magnified by the intelligence of the script, attributed to Keira's mother, Sharman Macdonald. She crafted a well-structured piece of storytelling that kicks into gear when Cillian's character William seeks the affection of Vera Philips—a nightclub singer, Keira's character, and the first love of Dylan Thomas.

Once William develops a relationship with Vera, the film jumps around in setting. At first, the plot kicks off in a London nightclub during a German air raid called The Blitz, taken from the German word Blitzkrieg—meaning "lightning war" from an etymological standpoint. In a militaristic sense, it's used to describe a surprise attack that combines elements of artillery, air assault, and close air support to overwhelm the enemies and their structured lines of defense.

For the most part, The Blitz was a skirmish of air supremacy involving the Luftwaffe and the Royal Air Force. The former force of inflexible immorality had previous experience in the air-raid regard, particularly when they attacked Poland just one year prior—the event that kicked off World War II as a whole. The characters in *The Edge of Love* experience this cacophony of battle all throughout the opening minutes before an explosion interrupts the ambiance of their bohemian nightclub endeavors.

After William is deployed into Greece to combat oncoming waves of relentless German soldiers, it's revealed he's begotten a son. While he navigates the massive explosions of the battlefield, undergoing some intense exchanges of gunfire and thus rising to the rank of Captain, his wife Vera raises their newborn child while suffering from the loneliness of wartime romance. She moves to a cottage in Wales, next door to Dylan and Caitlin, and upon his eventual return, Captain Killick greets his family as an emotional shell of his former self.

Not just physically due to the pregnancy, Vera is fearful that she herself has been overcome by change, and to the point of unrecognizability. However, she can't quite compare to the differences that define the new personality of her once beloved husband. Erratic in temper and impervious to romance, Captain Killick is haunted by the ghosts of the men he killed, beleaguered by the brutalities that he bore witness to on the battlefields of Greece.

```
Gravemen, near death, who see with blinding sight
Blind eyes could blaze like meteors and be gay,
Rage, rage against the dying of the light.

And you, my father, there on the sad height,
Curse, bless, me now with your fierce tears, I pray.
Do not go gentle into that good night.
Rage, rage against the dying of the light.
```

In terms of name value, Dylan Thomas—along with several of his pieces—holds far more significance than the movie in which the poet is portrayed by the talented Matthew Rhys. He didn't see action as Thomas, but in the same decade that *The Edge of Love* hit theaters, Matthew Rhys served as a WWI medic in the horror hybrid *Deathwatch* (2002). After serving as a Scottish officer in an entry called *Come What May* (2015), he's more than made up for skirting military service as the poet Dylan Thomas.

Unfortunately for Rhys, his co-stars, and the talented crew of *The Edge of Love*, their efforts went largely under the radar with regard to general popularity. Critics were rather harsh, as well. But the performances were praised, like Sienna Miller as Caitlin. At the 2008 British Independent Film Awards, she received a nomination for Best Supporting Actress.

Well-earned, and frankly, the other three leads could've received just as much acclaim. Alas, they failed to meet those standards in the eyes of pundits, as did the film as a whole. Meanwhile, *Perrier's Bounty* (2009)—the next film credit of Cillian's career—was a bit more revered overall, albeit not by too significant a margin.

Providing its narration is Gabriel Byrne, an all-time great Irish actor who appeared in a war movie in the exact same year that *Perrier's Bounty* hit theaters. It's called *Leningrad* (2009), and it features Byrne in the primary role. So does *Frankie Starlight* (1995), as well as *A Soldier's Tale* (1988). He's never appeared in a war movie with Cillian—their only partnership came with *Perrier's Bounty*—but Byrne's on-screen military service is nonetheless worth noting.

There are a couple of Cillian's collaborators worth noting in *Perrier's Bounty*, starting with Brendan Gleeson. After acting alongside one another in *The Tale of Sweety Barrett*, *28 Days Later* and *Breakfast on Pluto*—not to mention their shared credit on *Cold Mountain*—they had long been associated with each other's careers, in one respect or another.

With *Perrier's Bounty*, the co-starring efforts of Cillian Murphy and Brendan Gleeson established the Irish actors as a dynamic duo of modern filmmaking. Also among the *Perrier's Bounty* cast is Liam Cunningham, a co-star of Cillian's from *The Wind That Shakes the Barley*, along with another actor from that war film named Pádraic Delaney. Everyone among the cast of *Perrier's Bounty* puts forth hysterical efforts, and they all share a wonderful rapport with the next. There's a behind-the-scenes name worth noting though, as well.

Following *Intermission*, the dark comedy *Perrier's Bounty* also marked the second film from Cillian's career that was written by Mark O'Rowe. He's an accomplished playwright, who penned his second ever movie here with *Perrier's Bounty* and would go on to work with Cillian again. But for acting alongside one another in *28 Days Later* and *Breakfast on Pluto*, there's no doubt: Cillian and Brendan are the more iconic collaborators.

Another performer he's frequently associated with is the talented Elliot Page, with whom he starred in two movies in the exact same year: *Peacock* (2010), and *Inception* (2010). A psychological thriller by Michael Lander, the former is hardly worth delving into—not necessarily due to its dearth of quality, but its paucity of name value. As for *Inception*, however: That's among the most successful movies to ever feature Cillian, and on top of it marking his second collaboration with Page, it's also important to note that *Inception* also marked his third time working with the lauded Christopher Nolan.

As the writer-director, Nolan created an all-time great science fiction movie that will in all likelihood go on to be known as a classic. That can partly be attributed to the efforts of Cillian Murphy, along with others in the cast like Page, Leonardo DiCaprio, Joseph Gordon-Levitt, and Marion Cotillard. Several of those names had worked with Nolan before—*Inception* even features his most frequent collaborator Michael Caine—while it also marks the director's first collaboration with actress Marion Cotillard.

Next to Mélanie Laurent, she's perhaps the greatest actress in the genre's history, thanks in part to a starring role in a lesser-known movie that's titled *War in the Highlands* (1998). Next up for Cotillard were three co-starring roles in *A Very Long Engagement* (2004), *Allied* (2016), and *Lee* (2023)—in four consecutive decades, she's appeared in a well-made war movie.

Quite the array of war actors among the cast of *Inception*, but really, it's the behind-the-scenes work that's truly worth homing in on. The scale of *Inception* required hundreds of bodies on board for production, such as world-famous composer Hans Zimmer. He'd scored Nolan's prior two films, the beginning installments of his *Dark Knight* trilogy, and here with *Inception*, he creates just as imposing a score, evident by his nomination at the Academy Awards. He didn't manage to win, though—not like Wally Pfister, another behind-the-scenes name who frequently works with Nolan.

After shooting Nolan's groundbreaking thriller *Memento*, that famous cinematographer also operated the camera for *The Prestige*, as well as *Batman Begins* and *The Dark Knight*. He was nominated for each but the first, and arguably, he should've been recognized at the Oscars for *Memento*, as well. No matter, though. At the association's 83rd ceremony, Pfister was victorious for Best Cinematography thanks to his work on *Inception*, and it's easy to see why.

A mind-bending journey through time and space, *Inception* features insanely inventive set pieces that required the utmost forethought when moving into production. But when Nolan said action, Pfister fired on all cylinders and undoubtedly filmed his masterpiece. Careful shot selection, frenzied movements—across the board, Pfister's camerawork succeeded in making *Inception* a technical triumph.

At the Oscars, the team picked up three more awards: Best Sound Editing, first of all, courtesy of yet another Nolan teammate whose name is Richard King. But what's more, *Inception* was victorious for Best Sound Mixing, as well as Best Visual Effects. Four total wins out of eight nominations. It was even in the running for Best Picture, and justifiably so. Again: *Inception* remains one of the greatest movies to ever feature Cillian Murphy, and critics widely agreed.

Awarding it four stars out of four, famous pundit Roger Ebert cited *Inception* as the sixth-best movie of the year. Not the grandest of placements, but considering the caliber of its contemporaries like *Black Swan* (2010) and *The Social Network* (2010), the cast and crew should of course be proud of the work that they put into *Inception*.

One year later, Cillian would continue to toil away on film sets, and in doing so, he'd pick up further relevance in the grand scheme of Hollywood. With more notable placements among their respective casts, both *Retreat* (2011) and *In Time* (2011) feature brilliant efforts from the Irishman. Marking the first foray of Carl Tibbets as director, *Retreat* was co-written by Tibbets alongside Janice Hallett.

The second horror movie to ever feature Cillian—granted, some of his thrillers surely blur the line—*Retreat* homes in on his protagonist, named Martin. Showing up as his wife, Thandiwe Newton plays Kate, and the two begin the film by arriving at Fairweather Cottage, the only home to be located on an uninhabited island off the coast of western Scotland.

They're suffering from travails in their relationship after Kate went through a miscarriage, and now, they're renewing their interest in one another by spending a holiday retreat at one of their favorite founts. Run by Jimmy Yuill's character Doug, a ferry from the mainland is the only vessel with which one can reach the island. Soon after settling into the cottage, the couple's electricity goes out. They call Doug, then wait around for naught. Eventually, an unexpected visitor arrives to deliver some harrowing news.

Rounding out the primary cast is Jamie Bell, who plays Pvt. Jack Coleman. An exposition machine, Coleman kicks off the plot by informing the couple that a virus has broken out. Things unfold from there in hair-raising fashion, with everyone among the cast performing to the greatest possible extents. In back-to-back years, Cillian starred in two thrilling films, and of the bunch, *Inception* was likely the best. But *Retreat* is fantastic, as well, and it features an underrated performance from the actor at hand.

On top of playing a soldier in *Retreat*, co-star Jamie Bell put previous waves into the battlefields of cinema thanks to a horror hybrid called *Deathwatch* (2002). Not too acclaimed, but Bell led the cast, and in that same decade, he'd show up in a pair of all-time great war movies: *Flags of Our Fathers* (2006), and *Defiance* (2008). In the former, Bell served in a soaring depiction of the Battle of Iwo Jima, playing a Marine Corps private named Ralph "Iggy" Ignatowski.

In *Defiance*, talented thespian Jamie Bell showed up as Asael Bielski, a member of the Bielski Partisans—a unit of Jewish soldiers who traversed the Belarusian lines of World War II and recruited hundreds of Jews in the process. Second-in-command of the Partisans was Bell's character Bielski, while Daniel Craig portrayed their leader: Tuvia Bielski. Though not as well-known, *Retreat* marks Jamie Bell's fourth portrayal of a soldier, and he performs just as powerfully as the genre's greatest hero.

In the following year, Cillian upped the ante of his volume, and it began with a film called *Red Lights* (2012). A psychological thriller by Rodrigo Cortés, it sort of missed its mark upon release in terms of general success. But it remains entirely noteworthy for featuring Cillian as the lead, and in one of his all-time greatest archetypes: the physicist.

Marking his sophomore effort in that regard, Cillian has proven to be the undeniable champion of conveying physics on screen. Not that physicians work closely within a certain genre, or anything. But *Red Lights* continued that lesser-known trend of Cillian's, while remaining further worthy of delineation due to its ensemble cast.

While the war movies of Robert De Niro have already been largely touched on, a fresh name from *Red Lights* would be the actress Joely Richardson. Thanks to both *Shining Through* (1992) and *The Patriot* (2000), there's no denying her poise on the battlefield, even if her characters don't actually see any individual pieces of action.

In *Red Lights*, she plays Monica Handsen, while another notable name is the wonderful Toby Jones. A frequent collaborator of Cillian's, he'd later appear with cinema's war hero in a seminal genre title, while previously braving the battlefields thanks to *In Love and War* (2001) and *Dad's Army* (2016). Neither of those is too prominent with regard to Toby's career, but then again, neither is *Red Lights*, necessarily.

In that same year, Cillian had two other titles, both of which received greater acclaim overall. Written by Mark O'Rowe, the coming-of-age drama *Broken* (2012) is known as a well-made flick, as is *The Dark Knight Rises* (2012). Sure, he plays a minor role in the latter, showing up as Scarecrow for just a single scene. Not too noteworthy, but at that point, he'd been playing Jonathan Crane for the last several years. Regardless of Cillian's screen time in *The Dark Knight Rises*, it's still a well-known role within a high-quality film.

Given the status of *The Dark Knight* as one of the most financially successful films ever made, it only made sense that fans would rally in theaters to watch the trilogy conclude. Each of Nolan's collaborations placed Cillian one step closer to the center of Hollywood's map not just because they're famous around the world, but because no matter how large the role, Cillian always showcased true commitment to Robert Fisher from *Inception*, or the villainous Jonathan Crane from the superhero trilogy.

Of course, the series ended with *The Dark Knight Rises*, but for what it's worth, the Scarecrow lives on. His Cillian Murphy counterpart has stated that it became on ongoing joke around the film set that Scarecrow was incapable of death, always making it to the next entry in the series and often by the skin of his teeth.

His appearance in *Rises* is more of a cameo, but still, his caliber is on full display. He didn't read the whole of the script for *The Dark Knight Rises*—just his part, his one single sequence as the judge of a haphazard courtroom. He steals the scene, and perhaps that's because he went in with no context. Without a doubt, every entry in the Batman movies aided Cillian on his way to greatness.

Even *Broken* helped his claim to fame—a compelling plot and shocking moments will leave audiences on tenterhooks—undoubtedly aiding him on his steadfast path to greatness. However, in terms of achieving fame through strongly constructed stories, there isn't a property more important to Cillian Murphy's career than the prolific *Peaky Blinders* (2013–2022), a period show by Steven Knight.

For fans of the series, this is the definitive role of the actor's career, the peak of Cillian Murphy. And in full candor, considering the caliber of his performance in tandem with the quality of the television show itself, it's easy to see why the character has garnered so much respect. And, get this: Thomas Shelby is a certified war hero.

In the Bleak Midwinter:
Achieving Fame as a War Hero

Easing his way through the barren slums of Birmingham, England, a stoic man on horseback pays a woman to tell his fortune. After their brief interaction, some well-written dialogue reveals that the man is planning on fixing a horse race. It's an engrossing scene of seamless exposition, boasting a resonant atmosphere of industrial scenery, and as the man rides away on the back of his horse, steadfast and full of purpose, the dulcet tunes of Nick Cave and the Bad Seeds set the perfect tone for the entirety of *Peaky Blinders* itself.

Throughout six seasons of this famous period drama, for thirty-six episodes straight, Cillian Murphy portrayed lead character Thomas Shelby with an otherworldly gravitas, in a dusty black coat and with a red right hand. Gangster, politician, gambler, and businessman—a true multi-hyphenate, it's well worth noting that the formidable Tommy Shelby is also a former soldier.

Leading an ensemble cast, and even as a war veteran, Cillian Murphy finally achieved the status of household name. Not off the bat in the show's first season, or anything. But over the following decade, regardless of genre or medium, Thomas Shelby would become the greatest and most prolific character of Cillian's whole career. As the undeniable highlight of *Peaky Blinders* in general, he's one of the most endearing lead characters of twenty-first century television. And as the show's massive collection of devout followers would unanimously agree, he will forever be an icon of the medium.

NICK CAVE AND HIS BAD SEEDS

(chorus to the theme song)

On a gathering storm comes
A tall handsome man
In a dusty black coat with
A red right hand.

That can be greatly attributed to the world-class storytelling of the show's inventive creator, a British director and screenwriter by the name of Steven Knight. He's written high-caliber screenplays for such silver-screen projects as *Dirty Pretty Things* (2002) and *Amazing Grace* (2006), as well as *Eastern Promises* (2007). Some revered titles, and even then—against his critically acclaimed film-ography—*Peaky Blinders* is perhaps his masterpiece.

The opening season takes place in 1919, just a few months after the First World War had reached its dramatic closing point. Cunning crime boss Thomas Shelby leads a gang called the Peaky Blinders out of the lawless and squalid and atmospheric slums of the storied Birmingham, England. Meanwhile, the show itself is filmed in various cities across the lush U.K. landscapes, from Liverpool to Yorkshire, with the cast and crew also showing up to locations such as the Wirral, a peninsula in North West England.

For the characters in the show, the primary location of season one is a pub called the Garrison – the preferred drinking spot of the Blinders and one of the key places in which they (namely Tommy, the most astute of the Shelby siblings) conduct their business. An enterprise of modernity, the Blinders commit robberies and engage in racketeering, and occasionally, they dabble in illegal bookmaking. As a recurring plot point of the show's first act, the gang is also heavily involved with the local scene of gambling.

Showrunner Steven Knight was actually born in Birmingham, growing up in Streetly and consistently hearing about the past of his parents and their engaging stories from childhood. Viewing these tales in a mythological fashion, Steven took great inspiration from the formative years of his parents and parlayed that passion into the rags-to-riches story of the television show at hand. His mother and father—the latter a blacksmith, named George—were the primary fountain of influence for *Peaky Blinders* as a whole, but of course, the show takes its name from a real-life, urban street gang who ran amok in Birmingham for nearly thirty years in total.

Putting great research into their story, Knight brought a vibrant vision to life by virtue of world-class screenwriting, and the world of *Peaky Blinders* itself, its eclectic collection of characters and well-written plot points can be directly attributed to the creative genius of the showrunner. All that said—for essential as Knight's efforts were to the genius of Thomas Shelby, not to mention the show itself—Cillian Murphy is the name most often associated with the series as a whole. And justifiably so.

Admitting he was unaware of the real-life gang on which the show was based, it's evident that Cillian put great research into the notorious escapades of the Blinders upon being cast as Shelby. To great avail, but of course, everyone in the cast performs perfectly, with one of Cillian's many accomplished co-stars being the famous Helen McCrory.

She shows up as Elizabeth "Polly" Gray, the aunt of the siblings with the surname Shelby. As the treasurer of Tommy's gang, Aunt Polly played a prominent part in the plot for the majority of the show, and thus became a fan-favorite character amid the cast of *Peaky Blinders*. There's also Paul Anderson as Arthur, the eldest brother of the Shelby family, along with Joe Cole as the youngest, named John. Meanwhile, Sophie Rundle portrays Ada, the sister of the bunch.

As the leader of the gang, Tommy displays sheer authority in each of his featured exchanges, mostly by dint of the career-defining efforts of Cillian. Blurring the lines of good and evil, Tommy is an anti-hero of sorts, a ruthless gangster in one moment and a caring family member in the next. He's truly dynamic, and Cillian expresses his every word with the perfect intonations.

Even against the acclaimed efforts of McCrory and Paul Anderson, the Irishman exudes perfection in each of his featured scenes. Very few actors in history have taken the phrase "steal the show" and defined it like Cillian as Tommy. What's more, this is his all-time greatest archetype. No, not the gangster—the soldier, and in this case, a World War I veteran with PTSD.

As a Sergeant Major for the British military, Tommy fought in the front lines during the Battle of the Somme—the same excursion that included his supporting character Rag back in *The Trench* by William Boyd. For what it's worth, though, and again, that initial taste of battle didn't play out as planned. Before the Somme even truly began, Rag was blown to bits. Meanwhile, Tommy was in the heat of battle, the thick of the action, and even won medals for gallantry for his contributions to the War. He's constantly referred to as "Thomas Shelby, OBE," which stands for (Most Excellent) Order of the British Empire. A new-age knight, essentially.

Flashbacks from France give audiences a glimpse into the ever-changing psyche of the troubled primary character. A bona fide war hero, Tommy is capable in hand-to-hand combat, and he's an expert marksman who's hardened by the life of killing. But what's more is that the Birmingham gangster has the gift of gab to boot. He's always the smartest character amid any given exchange, partly thanks to some well-written wordplay from the dialogue of Steven Knight, but also by dint of the charisma from the show's leading actor.

As a vision of Steven Knight, the character of Thomas Shelby was seen into perfect fruition by Cillian Murphy. It's one of the greatest acting jobs in the history of television as the Irishman performs with a palpable passion, a purposeful poise, exuding pure poignancy as the plot's lead character—the powerful gang leader Tommy.

Although he'd never hurt them, even the lead's family can be painted fearful of his actions. He's a sheer force of the most cut-throat nature, both feared and respected by every citizen in Birmingham, and his grit can be traced to the hardships he experienced in France, in the bloody bouts of the trenches featured at the Battle of the Somme.

Considering the millions of moments of bloodshed that materialized during that infamous world conflict, it makes sense that Tommy would be affected. Physically, spiritually. Emotionally, more than anything. He's not easily harmed, and he's by no means religious. But Tommy is also bereft of most feelings—unless his disorder is triggered, you'll never see fear across his face. Unless his loved ones are harmed, you'll never see Tommy cry. You'll never hear him whimper or squeal, beg for sympathy or complain about his troubles.

He faces each of his problems head on, as after experiencing the despair of armed conflict, few other battles can compare. In tandem with the perfect understanding of the human condition, the Irish actor utilizes keen comedic timing and unparalleled charisma to truly showcase his range.

The same display of variety is featured in the show itself—running a wonderful gamut of emotion, *Peaky Blinders* deals heavily with various, hard-hitting themes, from politics and gang violence to post-traumatic stress and romance. Perhaps the most prominent fount of thematic resonance to be found within the show would be the interpersonal dilemmas of the gang on which it focuses.

The Shelbys are an endearing family, with each member sharing a unique rapport with the next. Siblings Thomas and Arthur pick on the younger brother John, and all three are protective over their beloved sister, Ada. There's also Aunt Polly, a source of counsel for the siblings, and until the final season of this world-famous show, each performer portrays their respective Shelby character with the utmost respect for its widely devoted fan base.

Also among the cast is famous performer Sam Neill, who plays the primary antagonist Chester Campbell. Throughout season one, he's devoted to finding a stash of guns that was stolen by Tommy and the gang. Hired by Winston Churchill himself, Campbell uses various tactics of violence to track down the weapons.

And for what it's worth to the history buffs out there—even if the show is more historical fiction, never true to real-life elements aside from the verisimilitude of the battles and the authenticity of its politics—*Peaky Blinders* does shine some tremendous light on the escapades of that famous Prime Minister. In the show, he's played by three different names: Andy Nyman in the first season, Richard McCabe in the second, and throughout series five and six, Churchill is played by Neil Maskell. They all show up to admirable extents as that figure of all-time importance.

This is an eclectic collection of characters, each with their own, engaging personas, with their own tragic backgrounds and their own tales of individual growth, and the whole of the family is haunted by the demons of WWI. Take Arthur, for instance. He isn't just a veteran of the War himself, digging through the trenches as a sapper like his brother – Arthur's also addicted to drugs. A nasty cocaine habit that makes the eldest Shelby a tragic character to root for despite his many flaws as a human.

The same thing goes for the rest of the Shelby clan – with John being a veteran, as well – each eliciting empathy from the audience for one reason or another. There's also Finn, the youngest Shelby member who experiences an arc like few characters on *Peaky Blinders*. But without a doubt, Tommy is the most endearing of the bunch. He's the most well-written personality that the show has to offer, a deep and developed portrait of battle, with each of his actions being deeply driven by the agonies thereof.

Behind his back—out of curiosity, typically, not with malice or to stir any pots—everyone discusses, inquiries about, or makes subtle references to Tommy's experience. They reminisce on his personality before he left for France, and how drastically it changed upon his long-awaited return. Dynamics of character are highlighted by the protagonist's escapades, with each conversation from every respective relationship always harkening back to the happenings of Tommy—his current actions in Birmingham, and his past travails in battle.

Pretty much every primary character to be seen in *Peaky Blinders* was created exclusively from the mind of Steven Knight, though he did base a few personalities off of those of real-life figures. Take Billy Kimber, for instance. He's played by Charlie Creed-Miles, and as the secondary antagonist of season one – next to Sam Neill as Chester Campbell, that is—Kimber opposed the Peaky Blinders by leading their rival gang, known as the Birmingham Boys.

A lot of names to cover, and they're all unique in their own respects while adhering closely to the style of the show. Aestheticized moments of violence color the streets of Birmingham red in nearly every engrossing episode, with varying emotions being elicited therefrom. Mostly, this is through the dynamics of the characters, as well as their well-written dialogue.

The audience will look to Tommy to confirm their every feeling, even when other characters are talking, and as the lead's demeanor is largely defined by silence, a je ne sais quoi soon develops around the air of Thomas Shelby that renders him all the more endearing as the leader of the show. He consistently drives the tone, no matter the tension of a given exchange—if Tommy is levelheaded, then so will be the audience. When not even on screen, Mr. Shelby's presence can be felt in every scene of the show.

THOMAS SHELBY

(writing to Winston Churchill)

Mr. Churchill, you should know that I am a former British soldier and if you look at my war record, you will see that I fought bravely at Verdun and at the Somme. Also, you will see that my actions at Mons saved thousands of Allied lives. I know that you resigned your ministerial position and the safety of an office to go and fight on the front line with the men. I read that you fought bravely, Mr. Churchill. Therefore, I hope I will be treated in any dealings we have with a degree of respect, soldier to soldier.

Thanks to his efforts in the Great War, the lead character of *Peaky Blinder* has earned the respect of Winston Churchill. After corresponding with him throughout the first two seasons, Tommy is even introduced to that famous Prime Minister. Series Two tells the tale of Tommy as he acquaints himself with a ruthless Jewish gang leader, whose name is Alfie Solomons. He's played wonderfully by English actor Tom Hardy as he joins forces with Tommy and the two gang leaders expand their respective operations across the south.

The season's final installment kicks into gear as the lead character prepares for his potential demise on Derby Day. After ordering the Blinders to steal the bet sheets at the races, the moment eventually comes. While Polly is dealing with the antagonistic Campbell, a few of the latter's goons—members of the Ulster Volunteers—kidnap Tommy and lead him out to a field.

Upon arrival, Tommy is given a grim presentation of his freshly shoveled grave. After taking in his impending fate, he asks the men for a favor: their permission to smoke a cigarette. He pulls out his signature matchbox, looks out to the distance, and through the whistles of the wind he monologues about his loved one. Then, he turns solemnly to his grave and embraces his long-slated death.

<pre>
                    THOMAS SHELBY

         In the bleak mid-winter.

              (Gunshots)

                    MAN WITH GUN

         At some point in the near future, Mr.
         Churchill will want to speak to you in
         person, Mr. Shelby. He has a job for
         you. We will be in touch.
</pre>

It's one of the greatest scenes ever filmed, no matter the form of entertainment, equal parts poignant, thrilling, and humorous, running a wonderful gamut of emotion and boasting impressive technique the whole way through. The sequence is framed and shot with nuance and ambition—boasting well-implemented sound design and authentic transitions of continuity editing—and after the scene's denouement, an indelible needle drop provides the perfect punctuation for the climax of the season itself.

Masterful strategies of technical filmmaking are on full display in every episode, with jump cuts and low angles accentuating the delirium of Tommy whenever his disorder kicks in. Editing can be used to elicit emotion from the audience just like a powerful performance or a well-written monologue, evident by the poignancy of the scene at the end of season two.

A dramatic fade to black, and by the start of season three—which picks up two years after the previous series of episodes—Tommy is now married to Lizzie. She's played by Natasha O'Keefe, and the season revolves around a rather thrilling prospect: a jewel heist, referred to by the Blinders as their biggest job yet. The treasure they seek is kept in the vault of a Russian gang, who hired the Blinders to provide them with weapons. These newfound friends cannot be trusted, however, so Tommy is the first to attack.

After several episodes, Tom Hardy makes a triumphant return to the show as the gang leader Alfie Solomons, and together, he and Tommy successfully rob the Russians of their many precious jewels. As audiences may have suspected, though, Alfie turns on him halfway through. In spite of his entertaining demeanor, Alfie too could not be trusted.

But with the life of his new son Charlie at stake—he's held for ransom, with the jewels demanded as payment—Tommy completes the job, and he does so the same way he won medals for gallantry in the war: by burrowing beneath the ground and making his way through a tunnel.

Amid gunfire at the Somme—or, beneath the action, if you will—Tommy was involved in a tunnel collapse, the primary source of his post-traumatic stress. During the War, specifically the Battle of the Somme, certain soldiers of the British army were assigned to dig tunnels underneath the battlegrounds, straight through the shadows of no-man's-land and into German territory. The soldiers who dug the tunnels—often deemed "moles" or "sappers" or more colloquially "clay kickers" —were part of the Corps of Royal Engineers, who've been architects of war since the days of William the Conqueror.

The Somme wasn't the first battle of WWI to utilize tunnel warfare, though it is the most noteworthy—this is by virtue of the numbers of sheer brutality associated with the river in general, as well as the manner in which the Allies forced the Germans to retreat. It was primarily thanks to the Royal Engineers and their tunnels, placing mines against the dirt and attacking German trenches from beneath. In a similar fashion to how he won the Great War, solidifying himself as a hero thereof, Tommy now uses his expertise at clay digging to help his fellow Peaky Blinders.

That said, he does recruit some old war buddies to tag along for the journey, en route to the Russian treasure of which multiple parties now covet. With the help of some veterans and their experience at the Somme, the jewelry heist resulted in a decisive victory, though not sans of consequences for Tommy. The season wraps with a meeting held by the gang leader that's essentially scheduled for the sole purpose of informing his family that they will soon be arrested for the crime. What's worse, they're going to be put to death.

Police storm the summit after Tommy doles out the loot they acquired, and the authorities then arrest the whole of the Peaky Blinders. Not Ada, though, for what it's worth. She's safe, as is Finn, who becomes a major character after appearing in minor fashion throughout the first dozen episodes. Aside from the two youngest siblings, the rest of the family is carried off to prison. To bring home season three and seamlessly transition to the start of season four—and thus marking the midpoint of the series as a whole—the majority of Tommy's loved ones are sentenced to death by hanging.

The announcement of their death comes as quite the surprise, both to the characters themselves and to the audience at home, especially when hearing the words stem from the mouth of Thomas Shelby. Member of the family, leader of the gang, and the figurehead of the heist. This isn't what the protagonist asked for, though, creating all the more agony in the psyche of Tommy Shelby.

It's an emotional plot point, the announcement of the death of some fan-favorite characters: the eldest Shelby brother Arthur and the youngest brother John, their trusted aunt Polly and their newfound cousin Michael. Those are four of the most familiar and entertaining personalities that the show has had to offer, and on death row—in lieu of the signature caps that typically adorn their head—the primary characters are now arrayed with nooses around their necks.

A gut-wrenching moment, no doubt there, but the tune of these four Shelbys had not yet been sung. Not in its entirety, that is. The fourth season of *Peaky Blinders* truly kicks off when Tommy is given a letter, and it's one from King George. His Majesty has ordered the Shelbys to be freed, no longer set to hang for their crimes against the country. But the experience on death row had already taken its toll. Much like Tommy experienced in the tunnels of the Somme, his family has now been acquainted with the unsettling face of death.

It didn't claim any victims, but the Shelbys are still affected. Particularly, Polly has started drinking (more heavily than usual, that is) and her son is now using drugs. Brothers Arthur and John are entrenched in the home life with their respective, loving wives, Linda and Esme, while Tommy and Ada are left to grab the pieces and put the family back together.

They succeed, for the most part, until making enemies with the Sicilian Mafia of New York City, resulting in the harming of Michael and the killing of John. Just one year after he escaped death by hanging, the youngest Shelby brother perishes, after all. Riddled by bullets with his cousin by his side, showcasing the brutality of the Mafia and the true threat of the show's fourth season.

The Shelbys mourn their beloved John, then proceed to get involved in the boxing circuit with series newcomer Aberama Gold, who's played by Aidan Gillen. An intriguing addition to the roster, and he's joined by his son, a pugilist named Bonnie who's played by Jack Rowan. Another first-time appearance on season four of *Peaky Blinders*—same goes for Adrien Brody, who shows up as the villainous Luca Changretta.

Of course, Tom Hardy reappears roughly halfway through the season. Typically the case for his character Alfie Solomons, a fan-favorite personality who helps the Shelby clan make their way safely to season five. They put a stop to the Mafia throughout the prior series of episodes, with the leader of the new criminal organization being played by the aforementioned performer Adrien Brody. An American actor and a bonafide hero of war movies himself, Adrien made a name for himself in Hollywood thanks to his portrayal of Władysław Szpilman, a Holocaust survivor.

For his performance as Szpilman in *The Pianist* (2002)—directed by Roman Polanski—the famous thespian was victorious for the Academy Award for Best Actor. That's one of the most emotional, influential, and greatest war movies of the century, and even a few years before, Brody put great work into the battlefield by way of *The Thin Red Line*. Another masterpiece of the genre, that time directed by the accomplished Terence Malick.

Adding great name value (and talent) to a cast of accomplished actors, Adrien Brody was able to shine through Luca Changretta's evil antics. And although his character was killed off before the fourth season of *Peaky Blinders* reached its close, plenty of other world-famous performers join the cast for season five. There's Anya Taylor-Joy, for example, along with Brian Gleeson.

The latter is the son of Brendan Gleeson, one of Cillian's closest collaborators, and here in *Peaky Blinders*, the younger generation shows up as the secondary antagonist of the show's penultimate season. His name is Jimmy McCavern, and he's the leader of a Scotting gang called the Billy Boys. Then, there's the primary villain of the season: Oswald Mosely, a real-life figure and leader of the British Union of Fascists.

A veteran, Mosely fought in the trenches of World War I as part of the 16th The Queen's Lancers, a cavalry unit of the British army. He and Tommy weren't entrenched within the same earthworks, though—while Tommy fought at the Somme, the antagonist was present at the destructive Battle of Loos. By far, the former character saw more action, as Mosely was rendered limp after injuring himself. Earlier in the war, he was showboating in an aircraft as a member of the Royal Flying Corps (RFC), and ended up crashing the plane.

He's not exactly a war hero, nor is he to be trusted. Much to his family's chagrin, Tommy aligns himself with Mosely, albeit with plans to blindside him. All the while, the protagonist is meeting with Winston Churchill himself, while Michael is now married and working for Oswald Mosely. Once Polly gets engaged and Finn becomes a more prominent character, the show shifts to its final chapter.

Season six features James Frecheville as a gang leader from Boston, named Jack Nelson, whose character is based on Joseph Kennedy Sr. Meanwhile, real-life figure Lady Diana Mitford is also introduced in season six, played by Amber Anderson. At this point, Tommy continues to hone his political prowess while also adopting another line of work. He now deals with opium, and recruits Alfie to help in his drug war against the Americans.

All the while, Tommy has become something of a family man. On top of his son Charlie, whom he had with his first wife Grace, he and his new wife Lizzie have now given birth to a daughter, named Ruby. Along with the likes of Jack Nelson, this new addition to the roster of *Peaky Blinders* characters makes up for a key figure who's unfortunately no longer featured: Aunt Polly.

Her actress Helen McCrory passed away while season six was being filmed, dying from breast cancer at the age of fifty-two. Aside from *Peaky Blinders*, other roles of her career included Cherie Blair in a movie called *The Queen* (2006), and in the final three *Harry Potter* films, she played Narcissa Malfoy. That's only scratching the surface of her eclectic list of credits, but even then, Aunt Polly in *Peaky Blinders* is among her most iconic.

It's revealed in the show's canon that Polly has been killed, deeply affecting the Shelbys in their own respective ways. Tommy had already attempted suicide to close the prior season—another testament to the demons still haunting him from the tunnels at the Somme. But as the plot of *Peaky Blinders* unravels in thrilling fashion like few seasons before, the lead character experiences a development arc like few personalities in television history.

Set in 1934, this final installment features the inclusion of Nazis, and Tommy is now interacting with the Irish Republican Army on top of his involvement with gangs from America. Parts keep moving from there as Tommy's daughter Ruby grows sick, and eventually passes away. Once they finish off the drug lords from America, the Shelby siblings get revenge for their beloved Aunt Polly, and Tommy kills Michael for conspiring against him. To end the show, Tommy passes the reigns of the household to his younger sister Ada, and by order of the Peaky Blinders, the series fades to black.

Over six seasons of critically acclaimed episodes, Tommy interacts with icons of the twentieth century who hail from Britain and beyond—not just Prime Minister Winston Churchill, but also Jessie Eden, a famous union leader, as well as Sir Oswald Mosley, the principal player in the British Union of Fascists.

A famous union leader, Eden is played by Charlie Murphy—no relation to Cillian, but she has offered her services for various war projects throughout the years. For instance: Along with *Peaky Blinders* co-star Paul Anderson, she appeared in *'71* (2014), set during The Troubles. Most prominently worth noting for Charlie Murphy is a miniseries called *Rebellion* (2016), in which she plays a medic during the infamous Easter Rising.

She exemplifies the craft as Jessie Eden in *Peaky Blinders*, while also worth noting is Andrew Koji as William Chang. There's Amber Anderson, as well, who shows up as Lady Diana Mitford. Plenty of those real-life names had been lost in the fine print of history books by the time *Peaky Blinders* premiered, with the work of Steven Knight introducing audiences to military leaders, war veterans, and fictional figures alike.

This show shined light on a widely forgotten segment in the rich history of Britain—the legitimate, real-life gang, that is—and when it comes to painting portraits of the brutal effects of war, few characters in the history of television have been as revered as Thomas Shelby. He's the show's main takeaway, thanks to Cillian's acting and

Steven Knight's writing, and across the board, the show excels at behind-the-scenes production.

From the ambiance of season one to the fireworks of season six, *Peaky Blinders* was lauded as one of the greatest television shows of the twenty-first century, and in the eyes of fans found everywhere, it even ranks among the greatest of all time. Endlessly creative in sundry tactics of storytelling, Steven Knight utilizes foreshadowing, implements red herrings, and teases the audience with cliffhangers to keep the plot at the perfect pace.

By dint of clever wordplay and well-developed characters, poignant themes swell to the surface of its plot, balancing out the sex, swearing, and well-shot scenes of stylized gang violence. And as subtext defines each exchange between these alluring personalities, their respective dynamics act as characters in themselves, evolving in every episode at a rapid but soothing pace.

None of that is to even touch on the show's impressive scale of production, the subtle dynamics of its sound design or the care that's put into its camerawork. The music, the costumes, even the intricacies of its editing—everything comes together to create an undeniable masterpiece, a series that in many respects became a worldwide phenomenon.

It boasts dozens of accolades across the board of associations that are committed to honoring the best of the television medium. Viewership, as well—upon the release of each successive season, the numbers would remain intact, if they didn't increase outright. And as you may have guessed, the show was a hit with pundits, who raved in their reviews ad nauseam about the cast and crew alike. For what it's worth, that's also happening here, and the majority of the praise in general can be traced to Cillian Murphy.

Much of the general audience's interest can be directly attributed to the allure of the Irish actor, too—the sundry emotions he seamlessly exudes as the endlessly endearing war hero. He's seen several historical figures come to life on the silver screens of cinema, and with *Peaky Blinders*, he did so again on television for an entire collection of gang members, a laundry list of politicians, and veterans of the battlefield to boot.

Among the finest shows of the century, *Peaky Blinders* was a massive success largely because of Cillian. It's the name most often associated with his career as a whole, whether analyzing his work in film, television, or with other endeavors like the theater. He's helped to produce plenty of products outside of the ones that most fans are familiar with, and much like the majority of his filmography, he deserves more credit for each.

After solidifying household name value for his stint on *Peaky Blinders*, this famous Irish thespian began to branch out a bit in terms of his overall career. He returned to his musical roots within several videos, even making his debut in that regard. What's more, Cillian contributed to the title song on *8:58*, an album by Paul Hartnoll that was released in 2015.

As for his videos of the melodious variety: Cillian debuted with "Hold Me Forever," which he directed in 2013 for an artist named Money. He continued honing his association with the music industry by appearing in "Stages" by Frank and the Walters, followed by "The Ways" by Allred Broderick and "The Meeting of the Waters" by Fionn Regan. Three more music videos.

With "The Clock" in 2015, he collaborated once again with Paul Hartnoll, contributing to the track by way of spoken vocals. And speaking of Cillian's old friends, the actor also returned to theater around this time with one of his closest confidants, the Irish playwright Enda Walsh. Their project from this period was called "Ballyturk," and it premiered in 2014 with Cillian as the star.

His character is unnamed, as are the other two personalities who appear in the plot, including one portrayed by Stephen Rea. A famous Irish thespian, Rea was first put on the international map of prominence through his performance in *The Crying Game* (1992), which was directed by his closest confidant: Neil Jordan.

Thanks to his starring effort, Rea was nominated for Best Actor at the Oscars, and a decade after *The Crying Game*, he teamed up with Jordan once again to help with *Breakfast on Pluto*. The latter title also marked the first competition between Rea and Cillian, with their next joint effort being marked by *Ballyturk*—the play by Enda Walsh.

Its story revolves around an involved discussion about Ballyturk, a fictional town from which the play takes its name. Some elements of magical realism rise to the surface once the plot kicks truly into motion, and across the board, the play was well-received. That includes the performance of Cillian Murphy, who arguably stole the show.

By virtue of his efforts in *Ballyturk*, the actor of the hour received his second nomination at the Irish Theatre Awards. Like his previous piece of recognition from that ceremony, the nomination was for Best Actor. And although he came up short for *Ballyturk*, the play features some world-class work from Cillian, as well as his frequent co-workers.

After that collaboration with longtime friends Enda Walsh and Stephen Rea, cinema's greatest war actor went on to appear in a pair of short films—even lesser-known than his stage plays—which were released in back-to-back years. Both underrated, as well, starting with *Harriet and the Matches* (2013). It was a vocal role, with Cillian's character being simply credited as "Cat." The following short film in which he appeared was *From the Mountain* (2014), then voicing the narrator. It was in the same year as the latter that he returned to the silver screen.

Both *Aloft* (2014) with Jennifer Connelly and *Transcendence* (2014) with Johnny Depp were released to little avail. In other words, they're among the least-acclaimed movies of Cillian's career, and generally unknown in the overall landscape of cinema in spite of some impressive efforts from Cillian. Like his endeavors with music videos, stage plays, and short films, neither *Aloft* nor *Tran-*

scendence could bolster Cillian's status as an up-and-coming superstar. That said, there are a few names worth noting among the crew of the latter title, such as Cillian's old friend Wally Pfister.

Marking his debut as a director, Wally directed *Transcendence* from a script by Jack Paglen. The famous cinematographer-turned-filmmaker made a name for himself by shooting six films for Christopher Nolan, four of which included the Irishman of the hour. The two were well acquainted before the filming of *Transcendence,* and that showed in Cillian's confidence in lieu of the numbers of its success. Audiences were higher on the film than critics, but even then, not even the name value among the cast of *Transcendence* could make any traction at the box office.

Nor could the following star-studded collection in which Cillian was a part, *In the Heart of the Sea* (2015) from director Ron Howard. One of the biggest bombs of its year, that historical adventure drama accrued just $94 million against a blockbuster budget of $100 million. But don't let those numbers fool you.

It's a compelling plot that revolves around the *Essex*, a whaling ship crewed by a company from Nantucket. The team sets out to partake in a whale hunt, but ultimately to no avail. After running into their prey in November of 1820, the ship sank solemnly to the mysterious depths of the expansive Atlantic Ocean, even further than no-man's-land and unable to call for backup.

The movie is based on a non-fiction book called *In the Heart of the Sea: The Tragedy of the Whaleship Essex,* which was written in 2000 by American author Nathaniel Philbrick. A historian, Philbrick was a finalist for the Pulitzer Prize thanks to his work on the maritime story, and he even won the National Book Award for Nonfiction.

According to critics, the film didn't quite do justice to the quality of the book. But it's the same story, tantalizing no matter how much the film potentially pales in comparison to Philbrick's original source material. Of course, it's non-fiction, based on true events, and in turn, the sinking of the whaleship Essex is the same story that inspired American author Herman Melville to pen his famous novel *Moby Dick*, which was published in 1951.

These characters are portrayed by such famous names as Chris Hemsworth, Benjamin Walker, Tom Holland, and of course, Cillian Murphy. The prolific American author and poet Herman Melville also appears in the movie, kicking things off by paying Thomas Nickerson for the rights to his famous story.

The last of the Essex survivors, Nickerson is played in the movie by Holland, while Hemsworth plays the ship's first mate and Walker shows up as the captain. As the second mate, Cillian portrays Matthew Joy, and he performs just as brilliantly as usual in spite of the implications behind the movie's success. Or, lack thereof.

Sure, the film adaptation of Philbrook's retelling holds nowhere near the name value of Melville's fictional story. Audiences were never going to line up en masse at their local movie theaters. But several of the cast members boast comparable name value to the *Moby Dick* story. For the popularity of these actors, *In the Heart of the Sea* should have turned the heads of film fans across the Atlantic and beyond.

Two of the Irishman's compatriots and collaborators are also among the cast in the form of both Brendan Gleeson, as well as Ben Whishaw. The latter has portrayed several soldiers throughout his cinematic journey, as well, such as historical figure Peter Llewyn Davies in a stage play called *Peter and Alice* (2013).

As a soldier, Whishaw always shows up with respect to war heroes past. Not quite to the extent of Cillian, though. Soon after the release of *In the Heart of the Sea*, the greatest war actor to ever do it made a triumphant return to the battlefield, grabbing his weapons and lacing up his boots and solidifying his claim as the best.

The Valiant Taste Death Once: His Triumphant Return to Battle

An entire decade subsequent to the release of *The Wind That Shakes the Barley*, the actor of the hour returned to the battlefield with the bang of a billion hand grenades. His fourth excursion in the war genre came by way of *Anthropoid* (2016), directed by Sean Ellis in what is in many ways his masterpiece. He conceived the idea in the early 2000s, then developed the screenplay further with the help of Anthony Frewin.

Parachuting into the German-controlled territory of a 1941 Czechoslovakia, exiled soldiers Jozef Gabčík and Jan Kubiš are tasked with finding their contact within their country's government-in-exile. After a crash landing in which Gabčík injures his ankle, the duo make their way to Prague and concoct a thorough plan to assassinate the capital city's *Reichsprotektoren*—in German, it means "Reich protectors," with their executive power in Czechoslovakia extending to include the Protectorate of Bohemia and Moravia.

Screenwriters Sean Ellis and Anthony Frewin take this inciting incident of two soldiers hatching their plan and parlayed the plot point into a full-fledged film. It's a truly inventive script, rhythmic in its writing and solid in its structure. The screenwriters had a vision with *Anthropoid*, evident on every page of its clean yet detailed screenplay, with tactics of both editing and cinematography laid out within the prose—mentions of cutting, as well as the camera itself.

```
EXT. PINE FOREST, HILLS - NIGHT
A man with his back to the camera. A har-
ness hangs from his back. A frantic reeling
action with his arms as he gathers in a
```

```
silk parachute. The action JUMP CUTS as he
buries the chute into the snow.
This is JAN KUBIS, 29. Strong slender frame.
JAN stands up into frame, his back still to
the CAMERA.
```

After spending many years with the story, Ellis added to his credit as a screenwriter by directing the overall production. What's more is that the auteur also sat behind the camera as the movie's cinematographer. Quite the undertaking for a single creative, and Ellis proved more than capable. But like marching into battle, it takes an army to make a movie.

Enter Cillian Murphy, who plays the Czechoslovakian soldier, Jozef Gabčík. Along with Jamie Dornan (a fellow Irishman) as Jan Kubiš, his character leads the plot through the annals of World War II. Specifically, the story homes in on the assassination attempt from which the film derives its title – Codename: Operation Anthropoid.

The target: Reinhard Heydrich, an S.S. officer who ranks high in the regime, orchestrated the Final Solution, and thereby helped to develop a diabolical idea called the Holocaust. He's an entity of true evil—deemed "The Man with the Iron Heart" by Hitler himself. Against all odds, and with a paucity of proper resources to be found within their reserves, the film's protagonists set out to stop the architect of evil, Reinhard Heydrich, who at the start of *Anthropoid* is already in office as the *Reichsprotektoren* of Czechoslovakia.

In order to properly execute a plan of this proportion, the soldiers of Cillian and Jamie are joined by Adolf Opálka, who's portrayed by Harry Lloyd. Also among the cast is Charlotte Le Bon, along with Anna Geislerová, and until the final gunshot of *Anthropoid* rings out, each and every thespian proves to be armed and prepared for battle.

In his early years, Gabčík was a farrier and a blacksmith. He even dabbled in clock making, while later in adulthood, he began working at a military chemical plant, and then, at a gas facility. After escaping a German-controlled Czechoslovakia and making his way to Poland, he then shipped off to France and joined the Foreign Legion as part of their 1st Regiment.

By the time he was recruited for the assassination plot, Gabčík boasted the rank of Warrant Officer, while originally signed on to help him carry out the operation was a Staff Sergeant named Karel Svoboda. After receiving an injury to the head amid one of their training sessions, Svoboda opted out and was replaced by Jan Kubiš. Probably for the best—while Svoboda was recovering, Jan proved to be the hero of the operation, as he was the soldier who threw the bomb that ultimately led to Heydrich's game-changing demise. Of course, Gabčík is now considered a war hero, as well. And with good reason.

Every plot point in *Anthropoid* unfolds in tantalizing fashion, a successful mission by Ellis who paid perfect homage to the famous pair of Czechs. He sang their praises with dulcet dialogue and a resonant tone of suspense, emphasizing the exegesis of World War II and leading his actors to greatness every militaristic march of the way.

Despite the praise the movie by Sean Ellis received from film fans, not many of them actually went to see the story of Jozef Gabčík play out on the silver screen. At the worldwide box office, *Anthropoid* was an absolute flop, accruing just $5.3 million against a $9 million budget. That statistic by no means does justice to the quality of the film, and frankly, neither does the consensus from pundits of the industry.

There are legitimate nuances to Cillian's performance—pay close attention to the expressions of his face, the intonations of his voice—and throughout the entire plot of *Anthropoid*, he delivers his dialogue with the perfect disposition. His lines are consistently defined by both witty wordplay and subtext, and no matter which actor he shares a given scene with, Cillian shares a wonderful rapport with each of his famous contemporaries.

It's among the finest efforts he's ever put forth: In one moment he's composed and contemplative—steadfast in his character's goal—only to change face in the following instant thanks to a newfound state of fear, melancholy, anger, or passion. It's a truly inspiring performance, but for some reason, Cillian never gets the credit he deserves for bringing Gabčík back to life. Sure, that can be attributed to the general dearth of name value that's attached to the film itself. But history buffs are familiar with the valiant tale of Jozef Gabčík, and they also know that Cillian's performance represented the soldier to a tee.

That's a historical figure of all-time importance, and Cillian showed great respect for the story by exploring its deepest details and parlaying his studies into a show-stealing effort. Detailing his understanding of the film and its many pieces of historical context, Cillian spoke about *Anthropoid* while undergoing media tours.

"The Second World War was such a massive, massive conflict happening on so many different continents," he said. "There still are incidents in it that we probably don't know that well, and certainly aren't taught in schools. I think this particular incident had not been well-known outside of the Czech Republic, hopefully, until this film comes out."

He and Jamie Dornan also worked closely with dialect coaches to help hone their Czech accents. Using his wit as much as his charm, the brains of Cillian are constantly at work with nuances to his performance, and the heart he displayed through each line of dialogue helped produce one of his most soulful overall efforts.

For many years, Cillian was considered by critics and film fans alike to be one of the best actors to have never been nominated at the Academy Awards. He eventually got the job done, even winning Best Actor outright. But of course, more on *Oppenheimer* in a bit. As for *Anthropoid*: He easily could've been recognized for his leading efforts therein, and frankly, he put forth another Oscar-caliber performance in *The Wind That Shakes the Barley*. In any other year, he'd have received Best Actor nominations for both of those efforts as soldiers.

Director Sean Ellis elicited one of his greatest ever performances, and as a whole, *Anthropoid* stands tall as a highlight of the filmmaker's oeuvre in general. After adapting his short film *Cashback* (2004) into the first feature of his career, Sean Ellis made a horror movie called *The Broken* (2008). He continued on with *Metro Manila* (2013), the most acclaimed movie of his career, and then revisited his script for *Anthropoid* and got the movie made. In the following decade, Ellis followed up with another horror film called *The Curse* (2021), also to great acclaim.

He's yet to lead any more troops into battle, and with the ending sequence of *Anthropoid* in mind, perhaps it's due to some post-traumatic stress. After the antagonist of the plot is killed and the protagonists go into hiding, their whereabouts are revealed to the Gestapo, the official and secret police of the Nazi party. A small squadron of Nazis torture the information out of Ata Moravec, who's played by Bill Milner, and with the location of the leads in mind, the Gestapo moves in for the kill.

The police plan to attack the lead characters Jozef and Jan, who are hiding away in Prague—specifically, they're holed up in the basement of the Saints Cyril and Methodius Cathedral, located in a district called Nové Město—or, The New Town. Their final battleground, the church is now frequently associated with the last stand of the war heroes in *Anthropoid*, even housing a museum in its crypt. The lead actors visited the exhibition, which is entirely dedicated to the famous pair of Czecks whom they so flawlessly portray in *Anthropoid*.

Justifiably so, as after all, they gave their lives to the cause—on June 18, 1942, the Nazis ransacked the Saints Cyril and Methodius Cathedral under the headship of Karl Fischer von Treuenfeld. In spite of being vastly outnumbered, the protagonists go out guns blazing, firing with every cylinder and holding the church's basement for six straight hours before eventually calling it quits. Bullet holes can still be seen plastered on the walls, and wreckage from the explosions still decorate the corridors.

For their efforts, a monument of Jozef and Jan was commissioned in 2008, which was constructed throughout that year then unveiled on May 27, 2009. It's located in Libeň, Prague, the city in which Heydrich was ambushed and assassinated, and in tandem with the museum that's been built in the lower story of the Saints Cyril and Methodius Cathedral, it's helped to render the names of Jozef and Jan as legitimate heroes of war who will forever live on in the pages of history books. Not to mention, the silver screens of cinema.

```
BANG.
The water from the hose continues to pour
into the crypt.The German soldiers walk
down the steps, guns at the ready.The bod-
ies of JOSEF, VALCIK, HRUBY and SVARC float
in the swirling waters.
```

As the shootout settles down, *Anthropoid* ends with a harrowing scene of suicide: The valiant Jozef Gabčík holding a barrel to his head. This was Cillian's fourth-straight war film in which he suffered a gut-wrenching death—sure, his character in *Cold Mountain* perhaps had that bullet coming. But even then, Cillian's performance elicited great empathy from the audience. At least, for a moment, before his character met his fate.

Perhaps at the peak of his powers, Cillian kills the role from start to finish. He highlights *Anthropoid* in its entirety, though from its cinematography to its sound design, the project is also adept from a perspective of technical filmmaking. It was even deemed historically accurate by scholars of World War II, proving that the commitment of the crew—mostly director Sean Ellis and co-writer Anthony Frewin—were just as pivotal to production as the efforts of its cast.

It's worth noting, though: In spite of its status as the best, *Anthropoid* was not the first movie to home in on Heydrich's assassination. The earliest example is *Hangmen Also Die!* (1943), directed by Fritz Lang, while others include *Hitler's Madman* (1943), *Men Without Wings* (1946), *The Assassination* (1964), and *Operation Daybreak* (1975).

The most recent retelling—released just one year after the depiction by Sean Ellis—was *The Man with the Iron Heart* (2017), directed by Cédric Jimenez. Oddly enough, it features another Irish actor playing Jozef Gabčík, and he's worked with Cillian before: Jack Reynor, who performs wonderfully as the Czechoslovakian soldier. His role wasn't as prominent as Cillian's in *Anthropoid*, though, a supporting role opposed to one of the leading variety. And while the Jimenez depiction of battle was relatively successful with critics, it came up rather short when lined up next to *Anthropoid*.

To be frank, it isn't just *Man with the Iron Heart* that pales in comparison to the quality of *Anthropoid*. From *Hangmen Also Die!* to *Operation Daybreak*, all of the aforementioned films to revolve around the assassination of Heydrich leave more to be desired than the subsequent iteration with Cillian.

That's one of the elements that renders him the hero of the genre: Each of the war movies in which he appears are of the utmost caliber. But what's more is that he boasts the quantity to boot. Though by no means a groundbreaking feat of filmmaking, *Anthropoid* is nonetheless a profound piece of storytelling, a high-quality war film with some tremendous work by Cillian.

Though not quite as revered, *Free Fire* (2016) by Ben Wheatley also features a memorable effort from the Irishman, along with co-stars Brie Larson, Armie Hammer, and Sharlto Copley. They all take part in a fictional arms-deal-gone-wrong, with Cillian's character Chris driving the plot as a headstrong member of the New IRA.

Set in 1978, just a decade after the Provisional Irish Republican Army was initially formed to end British rule—as per usual—*Free*

Fire was actually inspired by an event that took place during the Troubles. Along with executive producer Martin Scorsese, auteur Ben Wheatley (who co-wrote the script with Amy Jump, his wife) spoke with Stephen Garrett of *Rolling Stone* magazine and detailed his idea for the film.

The plot for *Free Fire* originated from a story Wheatley read about the IRA buying guns in New York and shipping them home on the Queen Elizabeth 2, a passenger ship used as troop transport in the annals of the Falklands War. Of course, no member of the IRA can be appropriately deemed a war hero, but Cillian's character Chris does partake in heavy gunfire for the cause.

Just one year later, he was involved in a massive military conflict, not the low-level war that came to be known as The Troubles. But first, before re-enlisting, Cillian appeared in *The Party* (2017), written and directed by Sally Potter. A black-and-white comedy, it's one of the most revered movies of the actor's recent credits. And while *The Party* by no means managed millions upon millions at the worldwide box office, the following film with Cillian proved to be a widespread success.

His return to the battlefield was under the direction of an all-time great figure of twenty-first century cinema: Christopher Nolan. It was the writer-director's first experience in the front lines, but luckily for Nolan, one of his most frequent collaborators had already mastered the war film. Of course, that would be Cillian. And on top of featuring the Irishman in a primary role, *Dunkirk* (2017) is also among the best war films under his ever-expanding belt.

He'll Never Be Himself Again: Becoming the Greatest War Actor

Before Jozef and Jan brought a victory to the Allies with their assassination of Heydrich, the good-guy coalition took several hits at the hands of the OKH—the higher commands of the Army of Nazi Germany, including names like Franz Halder and Erich von Manstein. Both of those nefarious minds helped to devise a plan called Case Yellow, which proved quite effective as the Nazis cornered the Allies in the climactic Battle of France.

After Germany invaded Poland, the French declared war on the latter country, starting in September of 1939 with their limited Saar Offensive. This didn't just kick off The Battle of France, but also World War II as a whole, and unfortunately for the Allies, they suffered a series of devastating defeats less than a year into the conflict. After a well-executed attack from the German Panzer Corps, the French forces found themselves forced firmly into a corner within some very familiar territory.

With Case Yellow in full effect, the Allies commenced a plan of their own: a tactical retreat called Operation Dynamo, which capitalized on Hitler's halt order on May 23, 1940. From the following day and until June 4, more than 338,000 soldiers of the Ally coalition—mostly those from Britain, Belgium, and France—were evacuated from the beaches of Dunkirk, a port commune with the third-largest harbor in the country.

Though a successful evacuation, Dunkirk was by no means a victory for the Allies. After all, they retreated, and were thus forced to abandon some key pieces of artillery on the battlefields of France. But there were also some heavy casualties on the side of the Allies—specifically, the British Expeditionary Force with nearly 4,000 killed and over 13,000 wounded. As one might expect, violence of that volume would take its toll on the soldiers who battled against the *Wehrmacht*. Take Cillian Murphy's character in *Dunkirk*, for instance.

To harken back to *Peaky Blinders*—the hit show that put Cillian on the map of international prominence—it's worth noting his character Tommy is directly referred to as "Shell shocked" on a couple of occasions, like with Sam Neill's character Chester Campbell at the end of season one. Some inter-universe foreshadowing, as Cillian's character in *Dunkirk* is credited as "Shell-Shocked Soldier" and goes unnamed throughout the film. Other sources call the character "Shivering Soldier," but still—Cillian's character is never truly identified, singled out only by the key component of his newly established disposition.

In his 2020 interview with *GQ*, when asked to speak about *Dunkirk*, the greatest war actor to ever live went into greater detail re: his experiences playing traumatized soldiers, saying, "I've played characters with PTSD a couple of times." Note the plurality, how he's not just referring to Tommy Shelby, but also to William Killick, the shell-shocked personality he portrayed in *The Edge of Love*, and perhaps even Johnny Boyle from *Juno and the Paycock*.

"So, I'm sort of familiar with it," he continued. "But all the veterans who went to see (*Dunkirk*) thought the whole film was very truthful and very representative of what happened." Critics called the film true to life, as well—even with regard to the eclectic array of personalities that encompass the combatants.

When asked about the relevance of the role, Cillian went on to say: "What the character represents is all of those men that came back from that conflict mentally destroyed. So, I felt a great sort of sense of responsibility to portray the character sensitively, and I did a lot of reading about it." It's evident in his performance that great care went into the role, and the same can be said for Christopher Nolan and the movie as a whole.

To conclude the *Dunkirk* portion of the interview, Cillian then discussed in great detail the genius of Christopher Nolan, his close friend and most frequent teammate of filmmaking. The actor said, "The hull of the ship that they find me on – they actually built all of that. That's the way Chris gets you to that place, because you're experiencing it."

This is among the finest war films of the twenty-first century, and perhaps of all time, and that can primarily be attributed to the intricacies of Christopher Nolan's mind. Critical consensus backs that up. And while it's undoubtedly the most famous, *Dunkirk* wasn't the first major motion picture to depict the infamous battle. First was *Dunkirk* (1958) by Leslie Norman, followed by *Weekend at Dunkirk* (1964) and *Atonement* (2007). All fine films, with the story even being formatted for the medium of television thanks to a show that was, once again, called *Dunkirk* (2004).

That said: On top of boasting more notable name value, Nolan's iteration is also the best. This is an all-time great filmmaker, after all, who consistently creates his plans of action with well-rounded tactics of the craft. For starters, first foray into battle features numerous actors among its star-studded cast who are known for appearing in his films.

There's Michael Caine, for starters, one of Nolan's greatest co-workers, along with Kenneth Branagh and Tom Hardy. Of course, there's also Cillian, and again, he's credited simply as "Shell Shocked Soldier." But speaking of Nolan collaborators: Perhaps the most notable names are those who comprise the crew.

Take Hans Zimmer, for instance. While it marks the most recent war film under his belt as a composer, *Dunkirk* was far from his first. In fact, Zimmer may be the most decorated veteran of war movie scores. His inaugural entry in that regard came by way of *The Thin Red Line* (1998), and he followed up a few years later with a one-two punch: *Pearl Harbor* (2001) and *Black Hawk Down* (2001). Those are three of the most famous war films ever, but *Dunkirk* may just be the cream of Zimmer's impressive crop. However, he's only scratching the surface of Nolan collaborators therein.

Edited by Lee Smith, shot by Hoyt van Hoytema—no matter the role, behind the scenes or in front of the camera, Nolan recruited his all-time greatest collaborators to see *Dunkirk* into fruition. Their efforts paid off in spades, as on top of its success with critics, this seminal modern war film also exploded at the box office.

Against a budget ranging between $82–150 million, it raked in just over $530 million in total. Pretty impressive, and after it cleaned up at the Academy Awards, the name value of *Dunkirk* soared to the sky like Tom Hardy in a fighter plane, the single-seat Supermarine Spitfire in which he spends the bulk of the film.

Speaking of: Though they don't interact in *Dunkirk*, actors Tom and Cillian have appeared on screen together a couple of times before, such as with *Peaky Blinders*. As recurring character Alfie Solomons—the leader of a Jewish gang—Hardy shares a wonderful rapport with Cillian after being introduced in the show's second season. What's more, Hardy is a veteran of war films, having appeared in both *Black Hawk Down* (2001) and *Tinker Tailor Soldier Spy* (2011) before he reunited with Nolan and Cillian.

He also appeared in two episodes of *Band of Brothers* (2001), and if you pay close attention to the climactic sequence of *The Trench* by Billy Boyd, you can even spot Tom Hardy carrying weapons in the background of a rather fast-paced shot. That hardly counts, though. In *Dunkirk*, he plays Farrier, and it's a memorable role overall. Like Cillian's it's one of his greatest claims to fame as a recurring soldier of cinema.

However, there is one more actor among the cast who's become a master of the war film. His name is James D'Arcy, and he's worked in the genre five times in total when it comes to the silver screen. Known for voicing Jarvis in a few entries of the Marvel Cinematic Universe, he can also be found among the cast of *The Trench*, even in a role that was larger than Cillian's.

The following war movie with D'Arcy was *Master and Commander: Far Side of the World* (2003), with *Age of Heroes* (2011) coming next. He played Ian Fleming therein, with that James Bond novelist being well-known for his service during World War II. Portraying Fleming gave D'Arcy grand exposure to the stories of World War II, with this one by Nolan coming next. Nearly every name featured among the cast of *Dunkirk* has put in tremendous work in the genre—not just Cillian, but multiple cast members are now practiced soldiers, and as critics widely agreed, their efforts bolstered the quality of the film.

When delving into the story, predominantly worth noting would be its structure. Told in non-linear fashion, the plot plays out to the beat of the route march of Tommy—no, not Shelby, but the protagonist of *Dunkirk* who's played by Fionn Whitehead—as he retreats from the Battle of France and makes his way to the eponymous commune.

Another World War II movie in which Cillian is included, *Dunkirk* represents something of a turning point in the career of Christopher Nolan. With the help of his recurring cast and crew, the auteur claimed his first nomination for Best Director at the Academy Awards. He perhaps should've won, but instead, those flowers were sent to Guillermo Del Toro for his work on *The Shape of Water* (2017). Another modern masterpiece, so, no real arguments there.

But *Dunkirk* was also well-represented at the Golden Globes, the BAFTAs, the Satellite Awards, and more. Justifiably so, as Nolan utilized all the recurring techniques that he'd become widely known for as a filmmaker. On top of his collaborators, he also made great use out of a non-linear structure—his first two movies were also told out of chronological order, those being *Following* and *Memento*, followed by both *Batman Begins* and *The Prestige*.

Now in the war genre, he tells the evacuation story from three separate perspectives: one from the air, another from the land, and the last from the sea. An ambitious approach, with various POVs being presented out of chronological order. Disobeying the scripture of film structure once again, Nolan continued his trend of innovative storytelling, and he did so in a genre that's typically grounded in realism.

That said—after establishing the existence of his consistently creative vision—something special was achieved here with *Dunkirk*. There's a particular paucity of dialogue to be heard within the film, but it progresses at such a breakneck pace that the characters never once skip a beat in moving the story along.

In other words, its plot is perfectly paced, and that can largely be attributed to the manner in which it's told. Not the witty wordplay of its dialogue or the thought-out arcs of its characters, but the madness of the journey that these endearing characters are travailing. Mostly, audiences will be entrenched in the madness of it all, trying to keep up with the dynamic shifts of battle as if they were thrown into the thick of the infamous beach itself.

Large-scale production value will thrill fans by itself, with the filmmaker's signature brand of intricate sound design facilitating his most explosive set pieces yet. Aside from the endearing nature of its script—for what it's worth, the movie still adheres to a strict structure of storytelling with an inciting incident, a midpoint twist, and the like—the quality of *Dunkirk* is often highlighted by significant shot value, smooth transitions, and an atmospheric score.

In lieu of dialogue, Nolan utilizes those behind-the-scenes techniques to keep the audience on their toes, as if they're dashing through a mine field of handheld shots and jump cuts. Director of photography Hoyt van Hoytema even toted around a 55-pound camera that was designed to shoot in IMAX, and what's more impressive, he frequently did so on the back of a moving boat. Like Nolan, he was entirely committed to *Dunkirk*, and his work paid off in spades after the movie's worldwide premiere.

While his contemporaries make their films from the safety of the trenches, Nolan sets up in no-man's-land and opens fire on the mold. This unorthodox style is apparent in every careful frame of *Dunkirk*'s well-paced runtime. A unique battle plan with proper execution. Even the narrative itself is markedly different from the majority of war films out there.

The events on the land home in on Whitehead's protagonist Tommy, while Farrier (played by Hardy) controls things in the air as a pilot for the Royal Air Force. Then, there's Cillian's character, who's stranded on a shipwreck in the middle of the sea. He's picked up by the Dawsons, a family of civilians who are joined by Barry Keoghan's character George. They toss a rope to the Shivering Soldier, who then leaps from the hull of his capsized ship—Cillian actually did the swimming—and into a boat that's primarily used for weekend luxuries, not shipping soldiers as they scurry away from battle.

To properly evacuate more than 300,000 soldiers during the real-life evacuation, the British Empire amassed a collection of 800 official casts. Assembled by both the Royal Navy and the Merchant Navy, these included a various range of vessels, like trawlers and drifters and other types of fishing boats. It was an all-hands-on-deck telephone conference as the Ministry of Shipping gathered ships from across the coast, with the majority of the most essential units being warships from the navies: thirty-nine destroyers, thirty-six minesweepers, a few corvettes, and even a cruiser called the HMS *Calcutta*.

With even greater numbers than the Navies could amass, private citizens rallied together and provided about 850 privately owned crafts for the cause at Dunkirk beach. From fishing boats and pleasure crafts to yachts and even lifeboats, this fleet would come to be known as the Little Ships of Dunkirk. Many of the vessels still exist, and in the silver-screen depiction by Nolan, roughly twelve of the actual ships were used throughout filming. Some iconic pieces of history, once again floating through the waters of Dunkirk, and now, Cillian Murphy is on board.

Deeply affected by the horrors he witnessed in battle, the Shivering Soldier grants audiences insight into the impact the brutalities have even on those who survive. Like Thomas Shelby from *Peaky Blinders*, this character digs deep into the human condition like few soldiers ever portrayed, and like most war films with Cillian Murphy, he absolutely steals the show with his pensive and pinpoint performances.

```
     The Shivering Soldier glances up. REALIZES
     SOMETHING...


               SHIVERING SOLDIER

     Where are we going?


                   MR. DAWSON

     Dunkirk.


               SHIVERING SOLDIER

     No, we're going to England!


                   MR. DAWSON

     We have to go to Dunkirk first.


               SHIVERING SOLDIER

     I'M NOT GOING BACK!
```

In *Taxi Driver* by Martin Scorsese, lead character Travis Bickle descends into madness due to his involvement in the Vietnam War. A few years thereafter, *The Deer Hunter* by Michael Cimino portrayed post-traumatic stress to a famous and revered extent, with the characters therein being affected by the same conflict as Bickle. Whether in retellings of history or in completely original tales, the Vietnam War has taken its toll on quite a few film characters throughout the years of cinema.

Other shell-shocked Vietnam veterans have included Charles Lane (played by William Devane) in *Rolling Thunder* (1977), and Ron Kovic as he's depicted by Tom Cruise in *Born on the Fourth of July* (1989). There's also Jacob Singer, who's portrayed by Tim Robbins in the cult classic horror film *Jacob's Ladder* (1990). That's still only scratching the surface of cinematic soldiers who are affected by the horrors of the battlefield, with even more examples materializing within the twenty-first century.

The whole cast of *Stop-Loss* (2008) are marred by PTSD, and in *Brothers*, one of the eponymous characters—the little brother Sam, who's played by Tobey Maguire—came face-to-face with death in the deserts of Afghanistan. He returned home a shocked shell of his former self, with post-traumatic stress defining his everyday life. There's also Casey Affleck's character in *Out of the Furnace* (2013), and Bradley Cooper as Chris Kyle in the famous *American Sniper*. All are accurate portrayals of the debilitating disorder at hand, but in the end, no one paints pictures of PTSD quite like Cillian Murphy.

```
                    GEORGE

    Is he a coward?

    Mr. Dawson looks sharply at George.


                   MR.DAWSON

    He's shell-shocked, George. He's
    not himself. He may never be
    himself again.
```

Intimate partner violence can cause post-traumatic stress, along with the unexpected death of a loved one, a debilitating illness, a natural disaster, and trauma related to childbirth. But by far, the life-altering event that's most commonly associated with post-traumatic stress takes place in Cillian's favorite film setting: the battlefield.

It was released during a flourishing period for the genre of war. On top of *Anthropoid* from the previous year, there was also *Darkest Hour* (2017), released a few months after *Dunkirk*. It depicts similar plot points about World War II, and to further emphasize its status as a deserving competitor, it's worth noting that the Joe Wright biopic was even nominated for some of the same honors at the Academy Awards. Both *Darkest Hour* and *Dunkirk* were up for Best Picture, firstly, along with Best Cinematography and Best Production Design.

And sure, *Darkest Hour* was victorious for Best Makeup and Hairstyling, while Gary Oldman was honored with Best Actor for his work as Winston Churchill. On the other hand—while *Darkest Hour* was recognized in two categories total—*Dunkirk* walked away with three wins overall, and two more nominations than its more dramatic counterpart. Pretty close numbers, but at the box office, Nolan blew his competitors straight out of the water and onto the shores of France.

From *Anthropoid* to *War Machine* (2017)—the former bombed at the box office, while the latter was released through Netflix—there's no doubt about it: *Dunkirk* was the most mainstream war movie from this prolific period of the genre. Out of eight total nominations at the Academy Awards, it won in three categories: Best Sound Editing, Best Sound Mixing, and Best Editing. It's also among the highest-grossing war movies ever—besting the likes of *Saving Private Ryan*—and it will always stand tall as one the genre's all-time greats.

Once he experienced the grueling effects of war in back-to-back years, Cillian went on something of a hiatus from the explosions and the gunfights. After working with Nolan yet again on *Dunkirk*, the actor appeared in *The Delinquent Season* (2018), made by Irish filmmaker Mark O'Rowe in his feature-length debut.

Sure, that creative is primarily associated with the neglected realm of screenwriting—this was first stint for O'Rowe in the generally desired director's chair, and thus the only time he's worked one-on-one with the actor at hand—but still, three out of four of the screenplays that Mark O'Rowe had previously penned are closely linked to Cillian's career.

First was *Intermission*, which helped put Cillian on the map. Next came *Perrier's Bounty*, the comedy with Cillian and Brendan, followed by the coming-of-age movie *Broken*. The only film written by O'Rowe that didn't star Cillian was *Boy A* (2007), directed by John Crowley. Quite the acclaimed project, but if the cast would have included Cillian, it would have been even better.

Just look at *The Delinquent Season* for affirmation. He comprises a quarter of the primary cast, with the other three performers being Eva Birthistle as his wife along with Catherine Walker and Andrew Scott as their friends. The movie kicks off in the home of Jim and Danielle—played by Murphy and Birthistle—as they eat dinner with Yvonne and Chris, who are played by Walker and Scott.

Both relationships unravel as the plot quickly progresses, and the intimate character study results in a high-quality project from the writer-director. It's a brilliant debut from Mark O'Rowe, though upon release, it wasn't exactly successful. Critics were lukewarm in their reviews—not the worst of scores, but even at the box office, *The Delinquent Season* fell short.

As did *Anna* (2019), an action-thriller by Luc Besson. It was widely panned, and barely scraped up the funds to recover the $30 million that went into its production. Not too surprising given the quality thereof, but *Anna* does feature its fair share of thrills, and considering the name value of the filmmaker in charge, one would think it'd have performed a bit better.

Known for his nineties stints such as *Léon: The Professional* (1994) and *The Fifth Element* (1997), some of the highest-grossing movies of their respective years were directed by Luc Besson. Even in the twenty-first century, he claimed further success at the box office by virtue of titles such as *Lucy* (2014). Not *Anna*, but no matter. Although it was panned by critics, a select corner of film fans did enjoy the experience, and with Cillian among the cast, it's easy to see why.

But to be perfectly candid, both *The Delinquent Season* and *Anna* pale in comparison to *A Quiet Place Part II* (2020), the first credit of the new decade from the career of Cillian Murphy. It's the second installment in John Krasinski's franchise of finely-tuned horror films, and although it couldn't quite match the success of the original when it comes to the worldwide box office, critics widely agreed that *Part II* is just as good.

Set against an inventive, post-apocalyptic landscape, John Krasinski's first foray into the genre of scares follows the Abbott family—Krasinski's character Lee, Emily Blunt's co-lead Evelyn, and their three surviving children—attempting to avoid a horrifying species of sightless aliens who utilize hypersensitive armored skin to wreak their havoc on earth.

Creepy stuff, and upon release, *A Quiet Place* (2018) was a massive success. Rave reviews from critics, great money accrued in theaters, and recognition at some prominent ceremonies—a sequel was inevitable, and (spoiler alert) they needed a new lead after the death of the protagonist. Time to call Cillian.

In his third horror film, he once again plays the lead: a coarsened survivor named Elliott who was friends with the family prior to the shift in the dynamic of humanity. To kick off the plot, he invites the Abbotts to stay in his headquarters, a safety bunker of sorts, only for Evelyn's deaf daughter Regan to take matters into her own hands. She sets out against the terrifying terrain of the *Quiet Place* franchise, and soon into her trek, she's joined by Cillian's character Elliott.

The two perform brilliantly as habituated survivors, with Regan being played by an equally deaf actress by the name of Millicent

Simmonds. She arguably steals the show, but if there's one of Cillian's co-stars from *A Quiet Place Part II* who's most prominently worth homing in on, it's undoubtedly Emily Blunt. This horror movie marked their first of two collaborations, with the next coming just three years down the line.

Among the most famous actresses of her generation, Emily Blunt is actually married to the writer-director of *A Quiet Place*. Her engagement to John Krasinski was highly publicized in 2009, and since tying the knot in the following year, the two have worked together in *Animal Crackers* (2017), an underrated animated film, followed by both entries of Krasinski's horror series. Just as she does in the first installment, Emily performs perfectly in *A Quiet Place Part II*, with Cillian replacing John as her co-star.

Though best known for his role as Jim Halpert on *The Office* (2005–2013), famous actor and filmmaker John Krasinski has appeared in dozens of high-quality Hollywood pictures. Some of those movies featured Krasinski as a soldier, such as *Jarhead* (2005) by Sam Mendes. But even on television, he portrayed a famous, fictional character named Jack Ryan, who happens to be a veteran of the War in Afghanistan.

He's only featured in flashbacks, but Krasinski nonetheless reprises his *Quiet Place* role in his masterful sequel, with another newcomer to the franchise being Djimon Hounsou. Thanks to *Deep Rising* (1998), *Constantine* (2005), and *The Vatican Tapes* (2015), who was a practiced horror veteran prior to his involvement with Cillian and company. Hounsou screams his head off in *A Quiet Place Part II*, constantly showcasing his prowess in horror movies—without a doubt, Hounsou should be known as one of the genre's greatest actors. He helped both Murphy and Blunt lead the sequel to greatness, and had put in great work well before its release.

There's a solid argument to be made that *A Quiet Place Part II* is the scariest of his eclectic collection of horror films. Gorgeous scenery and engaging set pieces are captured by some masterful camerawork, and thanks to Krasinski's script, *A Quiet Place Part II* is also a triumph of storytelling, a master class in pacing and seminar on suspense. It's one of the finest modern horror sequels, and it greatly bolsters Cillian's case as one of the genre's greatest actors. Aside from the battlefield, the wasteland of the apocalypse is Cillian's preferred setting.

His first taste of cinematic prominence was with *28 Days Later*, which came out in 2002. Nearly two decades later, he returned to the location in which his career was truly born. He has of course mastered other genres, such as science fiction. But no matter the given archetype—whether a soldier, or a survivor—he always steals the show when he works in his greatest genres.

He arguably does just that in *A Quiet Place II*, although, there's also Emily Blunt. She performs brilliantly, and she shares a memorable rapport with Cillian every slow, methodical, and barefooted step of the way. This was the first of their two collaborations, with the next title in which they appeared going down as one of the biggest films of the century.

But first, the end of Thomas Shelby. Wrapping up the arc of his all-time greatest character, the final season of *Peaky Blinders* premiered in 2022. There's a long list of accolades accrued by Cillian Murphy thanks to his otherworldly work as the dynamic gang leader, and to be perfectly candid, detailing them all would be quite the endeavor. However, there is one ceremony worth noting, and it's one that Cillian is quite familiar with: The Irish Film & Television Awards.

Since breaking through in cinema with *28 Days Later*, he's been recognized several times at his region's organization. Mostly, for his movie roles. For the category of Best Actor in a Leading Role – Film, he's been in contention seven times. That's one more than Colin Farrell, and the same as Brendan Gleeson. Plus, he's been nominated twice for Best Supporting Role – Film at the same ceremony. At the honoring of the greatest film achievements that his nation has to offer, Cillian was in the running on nine occasions in total.

Sure, he was only victorious for two of them. But that's just regarding the film side of that ceremony's award spectrum. On the other end, there's television, and for *Peaky Blinders*, he was nominated four times for Best Actor in a Leading Role – Drama. Of those, he also won two. A fifty-percent win rate, further shining light on Cillian's prowess when playing Thomas Shelby.

Throughout six revered seasons, he channeled whatever emotion would be called upon to fit the tone of a given scene – humorous banter with his brothers, or the one-sided rage of post-traumatic stress. Though not a film role, Thomas Shelby gave him tremendous experience when portraying a soldier of war. He parlayed that work into that of his greatest film role, for one which garnered him several pages in the history books of cinema.

In the following year, he showed up in a relatively unknown animated film. Not too typical for Cillian, and in fact, it was the first voice role of his career. Excluding shorts, that is. Called *Kensuke's Kingdom* (2023), it features a Cillian collaborator in the eponymous role: Ken Watanabe. A Japanese actor, he's portrayed numerous soldiers in both his native country and within Hollywood, with one example being General Tadamichi Kuribayashi in *Letters from Iwo Jima* (2006).

Marking his third time working with Cillian, the animated film *Kensuke's Kingdom* flew fairly far beneath the radar when it premiered in the year's second quarter. Not that its paucity of success was particularly effective to Cillian, though. Just one month after the premiere of *Kensuke's Kingdom*, the actor shocked the world with a blockbuster sensation in which he shined as the star.

It marked his sixth collaboration with Christopher Nolan, his second time working with Emily Blunt, and his first time being recognized at the Academy Awards. What's more, *Oppenheimer* was the movie in which Cillian made his triumphant return to the fan-favorite genre of war films.

Welcome to Los Alamos:
Playing the Father of the Atomic Bomb

After graduating from Harvard in 1925 with a bachelor's degree in chemistry—summa cum laude, at that—Julius Robert Oppenheimer tested the waters of several other schools (such as Cambridge) in an attempt to obtain his doctorate. The budding Master of Mathematics decided on Göttingen University, an institution in Germany, eventually graduating in 1927 and walking away with his PhD.

Alongside his mentor Max Born, the future father of destruction made tremendous contributions to the field of nuclear physics. An accomplished professor at Göttingen who had a hand in some statistical interpretations re: optics and solid-state physics, Max co-published a paper with Robert that detailed the Born-Oppenheimer approximation.

It remains the protagonist's most prominent work in the field of molecular dynamics, and after he was landed at the center of the scientific map, Robert went on to teach at both the University of Berkeley and the California Institute of Technology. During this time of mentoring future scientists, he also became invested in politics.

Chain-smoking cigarettes to balance out the stress, Robert is in a constant state of anxiety, and he therefore struggles to sleep. He rarely eats, and he invests most of his energy in his work—changing the world, one Chesterfield coffin nail at a time. He fuels his genius with smoke, capitalizing on each of his waking moments and earning his undergrad at twenty-one, a doctorate at twenty-three, and soon thereafter, Robert learned Dutch in a mere six weeks to utilize within his lectures.

These are just a few of his early-career achievements, but by far, he's mostly known for putting an end to the most devastating conflict in history – amid the tragedies of World War II, theoretical physicist J. Robert Oppenheimer created the world's first nuclear weapon. Wiping the sweat from his brow in the Los Alamos Laboratory – where he primarily saw The Manhattan Project come into fruition—and along with allies from the U.K. and Canada, he made an everlasting dent in history. His headquarters was located in the volcanic plateaus of New Mexico, where he created a device so destructive that it could end the slaughter of World War II with the measly press of a button.

The crew of the Manhattan Project are all well-represented in the depiction by Christopher Nolan. A star-studded cast shows up as these pivotal historical figures, such as an American named Josh Peck. He plays Kenneth Bainbridge, who was the Director of Trinity—in the deserts of Jornada del Muerto, the team behind the A-bomb tested their gadget of destruction.

Most of the primary characters in *Oppenheimer* boasted front row seats at Trinity: On the morning of July 16, 1945, more than 400 observers gathered to watch the "Gadget" bomb—designed like the "Fat Man" that was later dropped over Nagasaki. Another observer at the Trinity was Robert's brother Frank, who was played in the movie by Dylan Arnold.

Also in attendance was Benny Safdie as Edward Teller, the father of the hydrogen bomb, along with Matt Damon as Leslie Groves, the overseer of the Pentagon's construction and the director of The Manhattan Project. Both of those high-ranking figures were present at the Trinity Test, the site of which is now a National Historic Landmark.

Oppy called it Trinity after the works of English poet (and soldier) John Donne, and in many ways, the bomb test has outshone the work of that Englishman in terms of general name value. It's the biggest set piece in *Oppenheimer*, with world-class performers gathered around to witness the first detonation of a nuclear weapon ever.

Just as they gazed through their eyewear in open-mouthed astonishment as the spectacle unfolded, audiences will be mesmerized by these high-caliber performances from actors who were eager to work with the film's famous director. Rami Malick, Josh Hartnett, Casey Affleck, Florence Pugh—it really is among the greatest casts ever rallied for a single project, and many of the cast members even signed on without giving the decision one iota of thought. Like Cillian.

Though much was made of it this time around, *Oppenheimer* was far from the first time that Cillian said yes to a Nolan movie without even reading the script. At this point, the two trusted one another implicitly. Considering this is a war movie, Cillian had all the more incentive to say yes, but much to the actor's surprise—and to that of his co-stars—it's revealed on page one of the script that the perspective is first-person.

```
Peer into my soul- J. ROBERT OPPENHEIMER,
aged fifty, close-cropped greying hair.
The gentle sounds of bureaucracy...
SUPER TITLE: "1. FISSION"


                 VOICE (O.S.)

   Dr. Oppenheimer, as we begin, I
   believe you have a statement to
   read into the record?


I glance down at my notes.


               OPPENHEIMER

Yes, your honour-


            SECOND VOICE (O.S.)

We're not judges, doctor.
```

It's an inventive script from start to finish, careful in its structure and poetic in its prose. Unique for Nolan, as well, though he of course implemented several masteries that he'd been known for throughout his career—a non-linear timeline, an emphasis on practical effects. The English filmmaker knew the project was meant for his creative genius to design in the style that made him a household name in the first place. On top of those more technical elements, it's worth noting that Nolan also assembled his greatest cast to-date, or, as RDJ has referred to it: one of the greatest casts ever assembled.

Sure, there's no Michael Caine, nor is Christian Bale in the midst. But fellow Batman alumnus Gary Oldman makes an appearance, portraying the 33rd President Harry Truman and marking his fourth collaboration with Nolan. There's also Kenneth Branagh showing up in his third straight movie with the English director, while Matt Damon becomes a Nolan staple after playing a stranded astronaut in *Interstellar*.

Even behind the scenes of *Oppenheimer*, the creatives had great chemistry with Nolan, having worked with him on at least one film before. Composer Ludwig Göransson and editor Jennifer Lame had both contributed to *Tenet*, the prior entry in Nolan's filmography, while Hoyte van Hoytema was placed behind the camera—his fourth credit for a Nolan film.

Then, there's the Irishman. Though he's said that he never writes a script with specific actors in mind, Nolan has also told the story about casting Cillian as the lead, saying that after penning the screenplay, he saw the resemblance between his friend and the scientist while staring at the latter's picture on the cover of the book from which the movie is adapted. In the end, the power and charisma embedded in Cillian's performance was more than even Christopher was expecting.

In his 2020 interview with *GQ* magazine, before production on *Oppenheimer* had even begun, Cillian discussed ten of his film roles, and two of them were soldiers. He also talked about Tommy, a veteran and war hero. Four years later, just before the biggest award ceremony of his life, Cillian returned to the *GQ* headquarters to partake in another discussion. This time, the interview revolved entirely around *Oppenheimer*—his experience on set, along with his personal relationship with the personality he portrayed therein.

He cited the physicist as "intensely human," then went on to call him "flawed, contradictory, and fallible as the rest of us are as human beings." He had a keen understanding of Oppenheimer's demeanor, and he took the job quite seriously. Shot on location, the picture was also a passion project for Nolan, who relentlessly studied the creation of Robert's weapon—the definitive difference between a hydrogen bomb and an atomic bomb, how the former is actually more powerful to a nearly immeasurable extent.

Premiering in London, the bio picture *Oppenheimer* came out amid the SAG-AFTRA strike—the cast walked out of the premiere in an act of solidarity – a labor dispute that disrupted some of the marketing techniques of Universal, who produced the film. No matter, though. Clocking in at exactly three hours long, *Oppenheimer* was released to widespread praise from critics. And with good reason. From its sound design to its camerawork, every element of filmmaking is original in premise and thorough in execution. Just the script is praiseworthy.

```
                    OPPENHEIMER

Albert? When I came to you with those
calculations?


Einstein pauses. I watch raindrops make
circles on the surface of the Pond.


                OPPENHEIMER (CONT'D)
We were worried that we'd start a
```

```
chain reaction that would destroy the
entire world...


                    EINSTEIN

I remember it well. What of it?


                  OPPENHEIMER

I believe we did.
```

Upon release, the praise doled out from pundits to Nolan and his team was only overshadowed by the excess approval from film fans. It cleaned up at the box office; in other words, becoming in just a few weeks one of the highest-grossing biopics ever. Pretty impressive, but when it comes to the actual premiere of *Oppenheimer*, what's most prominently worth homing in on would be its correlation to a movie that came out the same day. Many months before the nominees were even announced for the 96th Academy Awards, the sixth collaboration between Cillian and Christopher became a worldwide phenomenon with the help of a little project called *Barbie* (2023).

Starting a Chain Reaction:
The Phenomenon of Barbenheimer

Like its biographical competitor, *Barbie* by Greta Gerwig was a massive success at the box office, accruing even more money than *Oppenheimer*, in fact. The former raked in more than $1.4 billion at the worldwide box office, while Nolan's war film made $962 million against a $100 million budget. These movies would have made magnificent money in movie theaters had they premiered on opposite ends of the calendar year.

However, they were both summer blockbusters, and they were released on the same day, which started a chain reaction for film fans who went to go see one of the films simply because they were also viewing the other. Enter, the worldwide phenomenon of "Barbenheimer," a world-famous example of counterprogramming in the realm of film distribution.

A portmanteau of the biggest films of the year, Barbenheimer is a combination of the titles *Barbie*, produced by Universal, and *Oppenheimer*, produced by Universal Pictures. But again, it isn't like either of those movies needed a boost at the box office, or anything. One of the most prolific directors of Hollywood blockbusters that the industry has ever produced, Christopher Nolan is no stranger to making waves in terms of the worldwide box office.

In total, his films have accrued over $6 billion worldwide. Of that number, Cillian contributed to $4.8 billion. With the exception of *Interstellar* and *Tenet*—two of the director's least lucrative titles—the majority of Nolan's blockbusters feature Cillian portraying one of their many iconic characters.

They're the greatest collaborators of the century not just because of the prowess they display when working alongside one another, but also because of their widespread recognition as partners of the industry. They're both household names at this point, and for some audiences, that's because of *Oppenheimer*.

From the moment its cast was announced, this biopic of an essential figure of World War II was destined for game-changing greatness, and frankly, so was *Barbie* by Greta Gerwig. Co-written with her husband Noah Baumbach, that renowned comedy was just as successful at the Oscars as it was at the worldwide box office. Not to the extent of *Oppenheimer*, but on the other hand, it did make more money in theaters.

Gerwig saw Nolan's receipts of $962 million and upped the ante by nearly $5 million overall, raking in $1.4 billion in total, albeit against a slightly larger budget than its *Oppenheimer* competitor. With Margot Robbie as the lead, *Barbie* is of course based on the line of children's toys of the same name, created by Ruth Handler and manufactured by Mattel. The fantasy comedy film co-stars Ryan Reynolds as Ken, the male counterpart of the eponymous plastic toy.

It's an endlessly creative project, and that showed with its numbers of success. With regard to the box office, *Barbie* was in a similar boat as *Oppenheimer* – everyone was going to see it regardless of its being released on the same day as the other. But the movies were absolutely bolstered by the other's respective release. People would take their kids to see *Barbie*, and history buffs could attend for *Oppenheimer*. And even then, they're of course high-quality projects, with even more hardcore film fans taking away some positives from both.

Over their opening weekend, the third one of July, both films were massive hits. Not only was everyone talking about them, but plenty of fans would even make a day out of the moviegoing experience, watching both titles back-to-back while hardly taking a break. Plenty of theaters around the world even held double feature showings, which only increased publicity, and thereby ticket sales. Quite the commitment for film fans to watch back-to-back blockbusters—and hopefully for their wallets, they attended the matinees.

Given the massive, three-hour runtime of *Oppenheimer*, theaters were even giving audiences a break between the showings. Granted, *Barbie* is significantly shorter, not even clocking in at two hours in total, but still. They're both high-quality pieces of storytelling with subtext and thematic resonance aplenty—a break between the movies gave audiences some time to contemplate the initial viewing, and if they watch *Oppenheimer* first and are now preparing for *Barbie*, the intermission also granted audiences a few minutes to smoke a cigarette.

With the amount that Oppenheimer smoked on screen (which is putting the physicist's habit lightly, in full candor, considering the real-life Bob actually indulged in a staggering amount of a hundred cigarettes a day), fellow addicts were undoubtedly craving a smoke for themselves.

On the opposite end of the spectrum of characters, nobody among the cast of *Barbie* has ever put a cigarette in their mouth. That's perhaps not true, but still—Margot Robbie and Ryan Gosling legitimately resembled their plastic-toy counterparts, with shiny white teeth and perfectly tanned skin tones. And of course, *Barbie* is primarily for kids. It's more palatable in length, and less mature in nature.

For as unalike as they are in style and tone, the two movies are commonly associated with one another, and it's easy to see why. From a standpoint of production—and even when looking at the history and backgrounds of the respective sources of material—there are many other similarities to be found between *Barbie* and *Oppenheimer* aside from their simultaneous release dates.

Success at the box office, sweeping at the Oscars—both of these feats have already been touched on. But a more bizarre fact is that both movies were also produced by similar teams, a pair of married couples: Christopher Nolan and his wife Emma Thomas were the producers for *Oppenheimer*, while Gerwig and Baumbach hold production credits on *Barbie*. What's more, they both deal with similar themes, like the idea that humans are directly affecting the state of the earth—a theoretical notion that encompasses the Anthropocene.

Among the strangest commonalities is that Mattel, the company that manufactures the Barbie toy line, was founded in 1945, the same year that Oppenheimer's creations wiped out the cities of Hiroshima and Nagasaki. Of course, there's also the casts and crew: Cillian Murphy and Christopher Nolan were to *Oppenheimer* what Margot Robbie and Greta Gerwig were to *Barbie*. The performers were plastered on the posters, and the names of some all-time great directors were finely printed beneath.

Same awards at the Oscars, as well. Both Robbie and Gerwig were nominated for Best Actress and Best Director, respectively. And although they came up short – Robbie to Emma Stone in *Poor Things* (2023), and Gerwig to Nolan for *Oppenheimer*—accolades at prominent associations aside—audiences around the world were bitten by the bug that was Barbenheimer, and that itch will forever be scratched by the history books of cinema. The portmanteau is part of everyday vernacular, and for several months, the stars of the respective projects were plastered on billboards, magazines, and article headlines everywhere.

Margot Robbie provided one of her all-time greatest performances as the brought-to-life child's toy in *Barbie*, with her previous portrayal of a figure skater in *I, Tonya* (2017) perhaps being the most impressive effort of her career. As for the Irish actor: his work as J. Robert Oppenheimer gives Thomas Shelby a valiant run for his money in terms of peak Cillian Murphy.

Just as the filmmaker led the actor at hand to greatness, Nolan made some substantial waves, as well, finally walking away with an Oscar for Best Director. What's more, *Oppenheimer* was even victorious in the category of Best Picture—not *Barbie* by Greta Gerwig nor *Past Lives* by Celine Song, not *The Zone of Interest* (2023) by Jonathan Glazer nor *Anatomy of a Fall* (2023) by Justine Triet. It was *Oppenheimer,* directed by Christopher Nolan with Cillian as the star.

And while those accolades were primarily accrued through his own doing, Cillian's performance undoubtedly played a part. He's truly hypnotic as he enraptures every thought of the audience, stiffens their muscles and steals their every breath. He and Christopher bring out the best in one another, and here with *Oppenheimer,* the dynamic duo didn't just bring a prolific historical figure to life— they also made history themselves.

A Very Proud Irishman:
Winning the Oscar for Best Actor

Up to the point of his sixth movie with his greatest ever collaborator, a simple nomination at the Academy Awards seemed to always elude Cillian Murphy. But with *Oppenheimer*, written and directed by Christopher Nolan, he wasn't just nominated for an Oscar. Thanks to his titular efforts, he even won Best Actor outright. There's a similar story with his collaborator, as well.

Prior to the release of his biographical war epic, Nolan received five nominations at the Academy: For both *Memento* and *Inception* he was in the running for Best Original Screenplay. With regard to the latter, he was also nominated for Best Picture, which was followed by Best Director (his first) and Best Picture for *Dunkirk*. Throughout the first twenty years of his career, while breaking box office records and garnering critical praise, Nolan was considered among the finest filmmakers to never win an Academy Award.

With *Oppenheimer*, he corrected those injustices with authority. Thanks to his seminal biographical war film, Christopher Nolan won golden statuettes for both Best Picture and Best Director at the 96th Academy Awards. With good reason. Officially among the greatest war directors in the history of cinema, Chris Nolan is beginning to give Steven Spielberg in that regard a valiant run for his money. The latter won the prestigious honor of Best Director for his work on *Saving Private Ryan*, while other war movies by Spielberg include *Empire of the Sun* (1987), *War Horse* (2011), *Lincoln* (2012), and *Bridge of Spies* (2015).

Still, though: Nolan and Spielberg are only scratching the surface when listing the most famous all-time war directors. There's also Samuel Fuller, as well as Oliver Stone—a pair of veterans, to boot. Some of Nolan's modern contemporaries have dipped their toes into war, as well. For instance, just take a look at the filmography of fellow English director Sam Mendes.

From *Jarhead* (2005) to *1917* (2019), he's made some of the biggest movies the genre's ever seen, and every time, he directs his actors to perfection. Here's the thing, though: Mendes has only written one of the war films in which he's directed, while Spielberg has written none. For consistently producing poignant and well-structured scripts on top of directing his actors, Nolan stands out for being an auteur.

Sure, Samuel Fuller can say the same, having written the scripts to every war film under his critical darling of a belt. But unfortunately, that American filmmaker was never recognized at the Oscars, while on the other hand—on top of his monumental success at the box office—Nolan's war films boast numerous honors at the Academy Awards, to boot.

In the previous decade, another one of Nolan's peers also won Best Director for a war film. Her name is Kathryn Bigelow, and at the Oscars she won for *The Hurt Locker* even against other high-quality war movies such as *Inglourious Basterds*, by Quentin Tarantino. The latter creative is an auteur, just like Nolan, and he was in the running for Best Original Screenplay thanks to his work on *Basterds*.

However, he came up short yet again to the talented crew of *The Hurt Locker*. That time, it was Mark Boal who was the winner, and just a few years later, he wrote Bigelow's follow-up war film *Zero Dark Thirty* (2012). That movie solidified them as two of the genre's greats, a status that Cillian would lay further claim to thanks to his work with Nolan. For *Oppenheimer*, the English filmmaker received a nod for Best Adapted Screenplay—based on the 2005 biography *American Prometheus* by Kai Bird and Martin J. Sherwin, this chronicle of J. Robert Oppenheimer has been rendered famous around the world.

Because they shone such beaming rays of light and passion onto the world-famous story of J. Robert Oppenheimer, both Cillian

Murphy and Christopher Nolan picked up widespread praise from pundits. Film fans. Passersby on the street. Everyone in the world was discussing this movie, and good or bad, that resonance bore fruit at the box office.

Prior to *Oppenheimer*, only one actor under Nolan's direction had been nominated at the Oscars. Of course, that was Heath Ledger for his otherworldly performance as Joker in *The Dark Knight*, and in the end, he even won the award. Posthumously, that is, as Ledger gave such a grand commitment to his character that it eventually cost him his life.

Just like Cillian, he had never won an Oscar prior to his victory under Nolan's direction. However, Heath was nominated once before thanks to his work in *Brokeback Mountain* (2005). He came up short, but still—Cillian had never received even the slightest of nominations at the prestigious Academy Awards.

Up to the point of *Oppenheimer*, all of Cillian's roles throughout Nolan's filmography were of the supporting variety. In *Dunkirk*, his role was even less significant. But in their follow-up war film, Cillian finally got to lead a film that was directed by Christopher Nolan, and he did so in his all-time greatest genre. If he wasn't the best before, there's no doubt now: *Oppenheimer* solidifies Cillian as the greatest war actor ever. What's more, it should also establish him as Nolan's greatest collaborator.

Christian Bale, Gary Oldman, Tom Hardy, Kenneth Branagh—since debuting with *Following* (1998) at the turn of the century, Christopher Nolan has amassed a devout stable of frequent collaborators. Those are some high-profile names of English acting royalty, and just as he's often considered when analyzing their respective careers, each of those actors are frequently associated with the films of Christopher Nolan.

However, for nearly two decades straight, from *Batman Begins* to *Tenet*, one performer stood tall as the director's best and most prolific collaborator: Michael Caine. He appeared in eight Nolan films in total, and each were roles of prominence—Alfred in *The Dark Knight* trilogy, John Cutter in *The Prestige*, and John Brand in *Interstellar* are all endlessly memorable characters, and that's primarily thanks to Michael Caine.

Of course, Nolan was leading him every step of the way, and that's why they're so often associated with one another. Not just for the volume of their work—*Oppenheimer* was the first Nolan film that didn't feature Michael Caine since they first collaborated—but also the quality of the actor's performances. Here's the thing, though: Just like Cillian for many years, each role of Caine's was supporting. He never led a cast, and that's now where the Irishman stands out.

It's a truly breathtaking performance, and it perhaps represents the best of Cillian Murphy. Although he's Irish, there was nobody more fit to play J. Robert Oppenheimer. They look a great deal alike, first of all. But Cillian also studied the scientist's mannerisms and intimately brushed up on his story, and that commitment shined through in his performance.

While Cillian's portrayal is undoubtedly more popular, American actor Sam Waterson previously played the lanky, obsessive scientist in a seven-episode miniseries—also titled *Oppenheimer*. Written by Peter Prince, it aired in 1980 to widespread acclaim, including a Golden Globe nomination for the talented Sam Waterson. But even in spite of that impressive performance, it's Cillian who will forever be remembered as J. Robert Oppenheimer.

He was armed and at the ready before Nolan could ever say "action," with the actor letting loose an otherworldly gravitas, a sense of absolute power that made audiences feel as if the fate of the world was legitimately resting in the palms his hands. Method acting came into play, as well, body transformation as he lost roughly two dozen pounds to accurately resemble the Oppenheimer silhouette.

"You had this hugely strong mind in this really frail body," Cillian said on *Jimmy Kimmell Live*, discussing the film alongside co-stars Emily Blunt and Robert Downey Jr. He was fully committed, and thus well-deserving of the most prestigious honor in acting. When announcing the nominees, former Best Actor winner Ben Kingsley spoke about Cillian in *Oppenheimer*.

"The performance is masterful, endowing his portrayal with layers of humanity, whilst his character created something inhuman. It's riveting to watch." It brought a smile to Cillian's face, and to that of Yvonne, his wife. A few moments later, the Best Actor winner from the previous year announced the victor for the honor at the 96th Academy Awards.

```
INT. DOLBY THEATER - NIGHT
After presenting the names of each nomi-
nee, famous actor Brendan Fraser announces
the winner of the sought-after award.


            BRENDAN FRASER

  And the Oscar goes to… Cillian Murphy.


The crowd cheers, and Cillian rises. He
kisses Yvonne, hugs Emily and Robert -
fellow cast members, and nominees - then
with a particular lack of vanity he
approaches the stage to shake the hands of
his Oscar-winning contemporaries.


Overhead, we hear:


              ANNOUNCER

This is the first Oscar win and
nomination for Cillian Murphy.
```

It's a truly touching moment, with Cillian rendered speechless after accepting the award. He took it all in, regained his wits, and gave a heartfelt response to the appreciation shown by an entire world of film fans. Beginning, he thanked his greatest collaborators (Christopher Nolan and Emma Thomas) for their twenty-year-long partnership, then showed his gratitude to the entire cast and crew with whom he worked on *Oppenheimer*.

Quickly thereafter, Cillian shined light on his fellow nominees, then moved on to thank the people he calls the closest: his parents Brendan and Mary, his partner in life and art Yvonne, and his two sons Malachy and Aran. Paying homage to the land that rooted Cillian in an independence of his own, he then concluded his speech.

CILLIAN

```
I'm a very proud Irishman standing
here today, so…
```

He raises his hand in victory, holding tight his golden statuette in lieu of a Mauser rifle. Time to bring in the sheets.

CILLIAN (CONT'D)

```
You know, we made a film about the
man who created the atomic bomb,
and for better or worse, we're all
living in Oppenheimer's world, so,
I'd really like to dedicate this to
the Peacemakers everywhere.
```

He exits stage left to uproarious applause, and after decades of watching our protagonist encompass an array of personalities, we finally fade to black. For now.

His passion pervaded the entire room of the famous Dolby Theater, and his heartfelt reaction was warmly received in nearly twenty million living rooms from all across the world. In all likelihood, it's a moment that Cillian will always hold close to his heart, forever remembering the 96th iteration of the Academy Awards. It was the most touching win of the night. At that same ceremony, however, the Irishman wasn't the only cast member of *Oppenheimer* to walk away with a golden statuette. .

Known for eliciting world-class efforts from generational talents, Nolan led two other actors to greatness at the ceremony: both of his co-stars on the Jimmy Kimmel show were recognized—Robert Downey Jr. was nominated for Best Supporting Actor, while Emily Blunt was in the running for Best Supporting Actress. The former performer even won for his work as Lewis Strauss, and justifiably so.

Following his work on *Tropic Thunder*, of all things—another famous war movie, a comedy hybrid that granted the actor immeasurable experience in the genre—*Oppenheimer* marked Downey Jr.'s second time being nominated for Best Supporting Actor, and his third piece of recognition overall. He finally came out on top, and Chris Nolan is partially to thank.

But even against some career-defining efforts from his world-famous contemporaries, Cillian Murphy stole the show. His efforts in titles like *28 Days Later* and *The Wind That Shakes the Barley* aside, this all-time great portrayal is perhaps the peak of Cillian Murphy. At least, on the silver screen.

The Academy surely thought so. At the associations 96th ceremony, he won Best Actor over some stiff competition: take Paul Giamatti, for instance. In *The Holdovers* (2023), that famous American actor undoubtedly overshadowed the efforts of his co-stars—the same can be said for Jeffrey Wright in *American Fiction* (2023), Bradley Cooper in *Maestro* (2023), and Colman Domingo in *Rustin* (2023). Against all those names, Cillian came out on top.

Previously, Giamatti had been nominated for Best Supporting Actor by dint of *Cinderella Man* (2005), a boxing film by Ron Howard. Though he came up short for a win, Paul was still accomplished with regard to the Academy—much like Bradley Cooper. He's one of the finest thespians to never get ahold of that little golden model of Emilio "El Indio" Fernández, with three nominations in the realm of Best Actor, and one for Best Supporting.

Meanwhile, despite their impressive careers in cinema, neither Jeffrey Wright nor Colman Domingo had been recognized before the aforementioned ceremony. Long overdue, their nominations were well-earned in 2024—although these movies were released in 2023, the Oscars took place a few months thereafter in March. As per usual.

In terms of nominations, it was an absolute sweep for *Oppenheimer*, which collected the most at the ceremony with thirteen overall. For working on six films in total and helping each other win their golden statuettes, Christopher Nolan and Cillian Murphy should be known as the greatest collaborators of the century. Sure, there's also Kelly Reichard and Michelle Williams, as well as Ryan Coogler and Michael B. Jordan, and perhaps the most famous director-actor collaboration—with regard to modern Hollywood— Martin Scorsese and Leonardo DiCaprio.

They've put indelible work into films like *Gangs of New York* (2002), *The Aviator* (2004), and *The Departed* (2006), along with *Shutter Island* (2010) and *The Wolf of Wall Street* (2013). But for *Killers of the Flower Moon* (2023), that famous duo lost across the board of nominations at the Academy Awards. To be specific, they lost to Chris and Cillian.

For *Oppenheimer*, the greatest collaborators of the twenty-first century were also well-represented with the British Academy of Film and Television Arts. It received the most nominations out of any other film at the 77th ceremony, and the same thing goes with regard to nominations—*Oppenheimer* was recognized in thirteen categories, and was victorious in seven.

It was also the most nominated movie at the 28th Satellite Awards, and the second-most recognized title at the 81st Golden

Globe Awards. Pretty impressive statistics, and none of that is to even home in on the individual awards that were doled out to Cillian. Sure, his Oscar statuette Best Actor—those history making efforts as J. Robert Oppenheimer have largely been covered already. Here's the thing, though: At all three of those other ceremonies—the BAFTAs, the Satellites, and the Globes—the Irishman won for Best Actor in a Film.

On top of the Oscars, this Nolan biopic also marked Cillian's first win at both the Globes and the BAFTAs—two of the most prominent award associations that the industry has to offer. Then, there's the Screen Actors Guild. At the 24th ceremony of their annual Awards, Cillian was both nominated and victorious for the first time in his career. Even still, that's only getting started with regard to Cillian's awards.

Quite frankly, the list of accolades he accrued for *Oppenheimer* could continue for a few more pages. But without a doubt, his Oscar was the most important that arose from his experience on *Oppenheimer*. And on top of being a memorable moment from Cillian's career, it was also a historic feat for his country as a whole.

With a long and storied history at the Academy Awards, performers from Ireland have been nominated for Best Actor since Barry Fitzgerald was in the running for *Going My Way* (1944). After that seventeenth ceremony of the famous association, eleven thespians have been nominated in the long sought after category of Best Actor, from Kenneth Branagh and Liam Neeson to Paul Mescal and Colin Farrell. Some names like Richard Harris have even been nominated twice.

Then, there's Daniel Day-Lewis. With three wins for Best Actor under his highly-lauded belt, he's the most winning name in the history of the category, not to mention someone who boasts the status as a citizen of Ireland. In that regard, though, it's worth noting that Day-Lewis was actually born in London. In other words, since the association's inception in 1929, only one actor born in

Ireland has won an Oscar for Best Actor. That would be Cillian Murphy.

Alright, enough about awards season—after Chris Nolan is touched on, that is. Like his greatest collaborator, Nolan had never been victorious at the Oscars prior to *Oppenheimer*. Sure, he'd been nominated, unlike Cillian Murphy. But at the Globes and the BAFTAs, as well, *Oppenheimer* marked a historic entry among Nolan's acclaimed filmography.

He'd previously been nominated for Best Director on two occasions at both of those prominent ceremonies. What's more, the recognition was for the same two films. The first materialized thanks to his work on *Inception*, and the second time, he was honored thanks to *Dunkirk*. Both of those movies feature Cillian, for what it's worth – after directing him five prior times, Nolan helped Cillian claim victories at all the industry's most prestigious ceremonies. And vice versa.

For both *Inception* and *Dunkirk*, the English filmmaker could've easily won a golden statuette at the Oscars, but it was *Oppenheimer* that eventually did it. Same thing at the BAFTAs, and at the Golden Globes. That's a lot of accolades to keep track of, numerous names of ceremonies and individual awards. All noteworthy, though. Badges of honor, each accolade accrued by Cillian and Christopher represent their grand commitment to the craft, their unrivaled prowess in the realm of cinema. What's more, it also shines light on their appreciation for veterans.

Both names put months of research into their respective lines of work. Look at Nolan's nights of studying, not just as a historian, but also as a creative. He pulled out all the stops of his iconic filmmaking style, utilizing non-linear narratives and intricate intensities of sound design to see what many regard as his masterpiece into history-making fruition.

There wasn't a more appropriate director in Hollywood to direct the story of Bob the Physicist—a great emphasis is featured on his aspirations as a mathematician, with Mexican auteur Guillermo del Toro once citing Nolan as "an emotional mathematician." He put great care into the details of Oppenheimer's efforts to spread his tale forever, and of course, Cillian was committed, as well.

Just as he put in research for his previous role as what we will now deem Bob the Physicist, the Irishman also studied the mannerisms of Oppenheimer, the history of the Manhattan Project, and the legacy of his character in general. This is partly why Cillian is the best—not just due to the nature of his performances, the way he controls a scene and steals it with every exchange, but also because of the positive light he shines on the veterans of the wars themselves.

He puts such care and respect into each of the soldiers he portrays that it feels to audiences as if he's seen some legitimate action, as if he was actually taking part in the gunfights, forcing his way through the tunnels at the Battle of the Somme. As if he was legitimately fighting for Irish independence, and as if he was actually in charge of creating the first atomic bomb.

The best performances of Cillian Murphy's wide-ranging filmography can all be found within war films. Except for Thomas Shelby, that is. It's a television role, but still of the utmost importance regarding Cillian's status as the best to ever do it. As a bonafide war hero, Tommy gave Cillian invaluable experience into the tolls that are taken from the battlefield, and he parlayed those years of work into his ultimate film role as *Oppenheimer*.

And on top of his world-class performances that can be found in each of his war films, all of those in which Cillian appears are also high-quality films themselves. They're each of the utmost quality, in fact—boasting an impressive volume of accolades respectively, though none to the extent of *Oppenheimer*—and even then, some of Cillian's war movies are still highly underrated. Hopefully this book will shine light on their caliber.

Cold Mountain, The Wind That Shakes the Barley, Dunkirk, Oppenheimer—some of the greatest war movies ever made have included the actor at hand, and on top of always providing effective efforts as a soldier, Cillian has the quantity, to boot. In that regard, *The Trench*, *The Edge of Love*, and *Anthropoid* deserve more respect. At least there's Tommy Shelby to bring the popularity some balance.

Among the greatest shows of all time, *Peaky Blinders* is Cillian's greatest claim to fame as a hero of on-screen battles. However, he's also appeared in seven war movies throughout his critically acclaimed career, along with one short film, and even a stage play. And considering they're all of utmost quality, he's thus the greatest to ever do it, the best actor that the genre's ever seen.

He's mastered other realms of cinema, too, such as horror and science fiction. It's just that he prefers to encompass the thrill and the agony of war, and since appearing in *The Trench* by Billy Boyd, he's gotten it down to a tee. While he isn't slated to appear in another war movie just yet, chances are he'll return to his genre of preference before his career concludes. He still has plenty of ammo left— enough gas in the tank for one, two, maybe three more forays into battle. Although he won the Academy Award, the full story of Cillian Murphy has yet to meet its end.

Some Point in the Near Future: Thomas Shelby on the Big Screen

After making history with his greatest and most frequent collaborator, Cillian worked with another creative whom he can call a close friend: a writer, named Enda Walsh. Most of their works have already been discussed—the Irishman previously worked with Enda on the aforementioned play *Disco Pigs*, followed by the stage show *Ballyturk*, which has already been touched on, as well. As for the former: Cillian also worked with Enda on the film adaptation of *Disco Pigs*.

Now, they've returned to the silver screen with *Small Things Like These* (2024), directed by Tim Mielants from Walsh's adapted script. The writer took the story for *Small Things Like These* from the novel of the same name. In turn, the source material was released in 2001 by Irish author Claire Keegan, and it's classified as a piece of historical fiction.

The plot is centered around the Magdalene Laundries in Ireland, infamous institutions that ran from the 18th century and into the 20th to imprison "Fallen Woman" who had dropped from God's good grace through their "loss of innocence." These women were kept in what were essentially asylums that were led primarily by the Roman Catholic Church. As for the movie: It homes in on the same plot, and with a star-studded cast portraying Keegan's characters.

Oscar winner Cillian Murphy stars as a coal merchant named Bill, while Eileen Walsh shows up as his wife, also named Eileen. The plot takes place toward the waning weeks of 1985, with Christmas soon approaching for these Irish characters to celebrate. Set in the port town of New Ross, the fourth-most populous city in the country, *Small Things Like These* kicks off at a local convent, where Bill Furlong the coal miner unearths some harrowing secrets beneath the surface of his town.

Oddly enough, Eileen Walsh—no connection to Enda, the auteur—actually shone light on the same Laundries in *The Magdalene Sisters* (2002), written and directed by Peter Mullan. In that project, Eileen played a fallen woman named Crispina, and reception for her performance was positive across the board. Now, she's playing Cillian's wife in *Small Things Like These*, with another primary players being the lovely Michelle Fairley.

Previously, she appeared among the primary cast of *Rebellion* (2016), which homes in on the Easter Rising. She was also in *A Soldier's Daughter Never Cries* (1998), followed by *Ironclad: Battle for Blood* (2014) in the twenty-first century. What's more, Fairley had also worked with Cillian on *In the Heart of the Sea*, with *Small Things Like These* establishing the two as surefire frequent collaborators.

Also among the cast is Emily Watson, who should commonly be cited as one of the war genre's greatest actresses. Primarily, that's thanks to *War Horse* (2011) and *Testament of Youth* (2014), a pair of well-received movies set in World War 1. Next up for Watson was *Little Boy* (2015), now taking place throughout WWII, albeit to lesser praise.

On February 15, at the Berlin Film Festival's 74th annual ceremony, *Small Things Like These* was premiered to widespread acclaim. In his review for *The Telegraph*, film critic Tim Robey called the film "a tight-lipped Irish drama even more suffused with sadness than the logline implies," and said that the quality is "shouldered with hypnotic grace by a very special Cillian Murphy."

On top of starring in the film, Cillian also holds a production credit, alongside four additional names. Of the others, two are most prominently worth noting: Matt Damon with executive credits, along with producer Alan Moloney. This is the former's second collaboration with Cillian following *Oppenheimer*, in which Damon played Leslie Groves.

A veteran of the genre, Damon played three soldiers throughout the 1990s, most obvious being the eponymous character in *Saving Private Ryan*. But well before then, he appeared as 2nd Lieutenant Britton Davis in *Geronimo: An American Legend* (1993), taking part in the Apache Wars. That was followed by *Courage Under Fire*, in which he played a specialist named Andrew Ilario. Co-starring with the greatest to ever do it, Matt Damon proved to still be capable of battle in *Oppenheimer*. And clearly, he and Cillian didn't just share a wonderful chemistry as actors, considering they collaborated again just one year later.

What's more, *Small Things Like These* marks the third time that Alan Moloney worked with Cillian Murphy. He'd previously helped to produce both *Breakfast on Pluto* and *Perrier's Bounty*, and now, Moloney seems to be a key component of Cillian's future career. In February of 2024—the same month that *Small Things Like These* premiered for Berlin to see—the two creatives announced the launch of Big Things Films, an independent production company.

Following *Small Things,* their next film is set to be released exclusively on Netflix under the title *Steve*. It's set in 1996, and follows the head teacher (played by Cillian) of an all-boys reform school on the southwestern outskirts of England. On the website for Big Thing Films, the film is described to be in the phase of pre-production, which typically means that they're still in the planning process.

But the script has already been written, adapted by Max Porter from his novel *Shy*, which was published in 2023. Previously, the writer had worked with Cillian on two occasions, the first with a stage play, called *Grief is the Thing with Feathers* (2019). It was penned by Porter and directed by Enda Walsh, based on the former's novel of the same name.

As a bereaved husband, Cillian won an Irish Times Theater Award for Best Actor, which he'd previously been nominated twice under Walsh's direction. For *Misterman* (2011), he even won as lead character Thomas Magill. Now that Cillian is working with both Porter and Walsh on a movie, in tandem with his production partner Alan Moloney, big things are clearly in the future for the Oscar-winning Irishman.

What's more is that he's set to produce *28 Years Later*, in which he'll also reprise his fan-favorite role as Jim, the bicycle courier, apocalypse survivor, and protagonist of the franchise's first installment. Horror hounds and film buffs alike would be ecstatic for his return, as his performance for many fans is a highlight of *28 Days* itself.

Along with Cillian as Jim, it'll feature several new characters played by the likes of Jodie Comer and Aaron Taylor-Johnson. There's also a pair of Englishmen in Jack O'Connell and Ralph Fiennes, with those two newcomers having put greater work into war films that the majority of their contemporaries. The former led *Private Peaceful* (2012) to relative acclaim, and just two years later, he appeared as WWII veteran Louis Zamperini in a movie called *Unbroken* (2014).

Most recently, O'Connell started playing a stoic soldier named Lieutenant Paddy Mayne, who helped David Sterling establish the Special Air Service unit of the British Army in World War II. Both figures have been forgotten in the many pages of their country's history books, with O'Connell shining tremendous light on his lionhearted compatriots. What's more, he also played Jan Kubiš in *The Man with the Iron Heart* (2017). Quite the coincidence there, as Cillian had previously played Jan's good friend Jozef Gabčík.

Perhaps the best war movie under O'Connell's impressive, webbed belt is *'71* (2014), in which he plays a fictional soldier by the name of Gary Hook. It's among the best movies of its year, granting war fans a glimpse into Northern Ireland's infamous conflict, The Troubles. Taking place just a couple of years after The Troubles kicked into gear, *'71* features a witty screenplay facilitating some truly memorable performances from an underrated cast.

Two of Cillian's contemporaries are featured with O'Connell, as both Barry Keoghan and Paul Anderson have played numerous soldiers throughout their career. Oftentimes, they served alongside Cillian. Though not a war movie, *28 Years* will mark O'Connell's first collaboration with the Irishman, and the same thing goes for Fiennes.

As for Ralph Fiennes and the war genre: movies like *Schindler's List* (1993) and *The English Patient* (1996) are among the greatest ever made, and he co-stars in them both. They're also his only two nominations at the Academy Awards, but another movie worth noting is *The Hurt Locker* (2009), in which Fiennes provides a supporting performance under Kathryn Bigelow's direction. Those are three of the greatest war movies ever produced—with a bit more output, Fiennes would be in discussion as the genre's greatest veteran.

Now, he'll traverse the apocalypse with the war hero himself. This is among Cillian's greatest roles to date, and he's set to appear in a "surprising way" according to executive producer Tom Rothman. Quite exciting, with some fans speculating that Jim will return to the wasteland this time as a zombie. It'll remind fans how well he portrayed the survivor so early in his career, but no matter how many times he may reprise the character Jim, there's no doubt about the true icon from Cillian's career.

While his award-winning efforts as J. Robert Oppenheimer marked the peak of Cillian's acclaimed career in cinema, he'll always be remembered for Thomas Shelby, the indelible personality and bonafide war hero whom he brought to life on television. In hindsight, it's a marvel to consider that Steven Knight was considering Jason Statham to play Tommy in lieu of Cillian Murphy. Perhaps it's because the latter had never even heard of the real-life gang before he was handed a script.

It's a good thing that Cillian was able to persuade the showrunner, though, as the Irishman brought to brilliant life the intricacies of Steven Knight's masterpiece, rendering Thomas Shelby a household name in the process. Much of the loyalty of the *Peaky Blind-*

ers fan base can be attributed to the lead's appearance, his rough demeanor and way with words, and of course, the show's devout following can also be traced to the efforts of Cillian Murphy.

Sidenote: Whoever tattooed Thomas Shelby on the inner linings of Dave Bautista's thigh is either immensely proud of their work, or embarrassed it ever happened. Ten pounds says it's the latter, unless he's a follower of the Peaky Blinders himself. The show boasts a massive collection of die-hard devotees, with the fan-favorite and critically acclaimed *Peaky Blinders* going down as one of the greatest entries of twenty-first century television.

At this point, the everlasting story of the infamous *Peaky Blinders* has come to a resonant close. The show had its acclaimed run for six sensational seasons, and Cillian was the star of every well-produced episode. He also led the cast of *Oppenheimer* as the eponymous, real-life physicist, and starred in the biopic *Anthropoid* as the legendary Jozef Gabčík.

He played an Irish soldier named Damien in *The Wind That Shakes the Barley*, and also a casualty of shell shock in the titular battle of *Dunkirk*. There's also Pte. Rag Rookwood, a supporting character in *The Trench*, along with the dynamic Bardolph who can be found in *Cold Mountain*. Every time, he's shown respect for real-life soldiers from world conflicts past.

He's learned conversational French, which he utilizes as Thomas Shelby throughout the final installment of *Peaky Blinders*, and even speaks a bit of Dutch as J. Robert Oppenheimer. He's always in harmony with his co-stars, and individually, his performances force the audience to consider the emotional profundity of his soldiers while also contemplating the nuances of their respective forms of suffering.

And for as seriously as Cillian takes his all-encompassing line of work, he's also a committed family man. In 2006, he married his longtime girlfriend Yvonne McGuinness, a visual artist who was born in Kilkenny, Ireland. Together, Cillian and Yvonne have two sons: Malachy, born in 2005, and Aran, who's two years his brother's junior. They're constant founts of inspiration to Cillian as he defines an entire generation of performers through his wide-ranging career.

Though Cillian can play characters of any archetype and within whatever genre he may choose, he shines brightest in combat zones, with his work putting his co-workers in the grim shades of the battlefield. When accounting for his career-defining work as war hero Thomas Shelby, there should be no doubt left when it comes to cinema's history books—in the annals of war movies, the greatest actor has a name, and that name is Cillian Murphy.